The Silence of Unknowing

~

THE KEY TO THE SPIRITUAL LIFE

Terence Grant

TRIUMPH™ BOOKS
Liguori, Missouri

Published by Triumph™ Books
Liguori, Missouri
An Imprint of Liguori Publications

Library of Congress Cataloging-in-Publication Data

Grant, Terence.
    The silence of unknowing : the key to the spiritual life / Terence Grant.
       p.   cm.
    Includes bibliographical references.
    ISBN 0-89243-828-2
    1. Spiritual life—Catholic Church. 2. Catholic Church—Doctrines.
I. Title.
    BX2350.2.G694 1995
    248.4'82—dc20   95-10762

Acknowledgments

~

I want to express my deep gratitude to the people and the parish communities to whom these talks were first given. It was out of my relationship to them that the material in this book was inspired.

Contents

~

Foreword ~ vii

1. The Desire to Become ~ 1

2. How Do We Change? ~ 11

3. Turnaround ~ 23

4. The Really Good News ~ 29

5. The Courage to Search ~ 35

6. Self-Awareness ~ 41

7. What's Our Motivation? ~ 47

8. Transforming Our Vision ~ 53

9. Healing Our Source Relationship ~ 59

10. Kindness from the Beginning ~ 65

11. Know Yourself ~ 71

12. Death and New Life ~ 77

13. A Firsthand Faith ~ 83

14. The Silence of Unknowing ~ 91

15. The True Shepherd ~ 97

16. The Illusion of Separateness ~ 101

17. One in the Spirit ~ 107

18. The Ripple Effect ~ 113

19. Present-Moment Living ~ 119

20. Listening to the Inner Voice ~ 125

21. The God of the Now ~ 131

22. The Real Miracle ~ 137

23. The Sunday Bargain ~ 143

24. "God Help Us If We Got What We Deserve!" ~ 149

25. The Dark Night ~ 155

26. True Freedom ~ 161

27. A Moment of Grace ~ 173

Postscript ~ 179

Appendix I: Some Practical Meditations ~ 181

Appendix II: Methods of Listening Prayer ~ 187

Notes ~ 193

About the Author ~ 199

Foreword

~

This book evolved out of my years in ministry—preaching, giving talks at workshops, or leading contemplative weekends. I don't pretend to be a perfected spiritual master. I continue to grow, to confront illusion and ignorance as obstacles in my life. However, I have written in this book about my own authentic spiritual experience on a path that has led me to growing liberation from anger and fear. I hope this book will help you, the reader, to find your own healing and freedom on your own version of this path.

I have included in the book a number of stories and practical examples intended to illustrate concretely the sometimes intense material under discussion. Many of these illustrations arose out of my personal experiences, or my experiences in parish ministry. Where necessary, I have modified the details of these illustrations to preserve the anonymity of the people involved. I also cite scriptural episodes to illuminate the issue under discussion in each chapter.

I want to sound an important note of caution in this Foreword: This book is not a gospel that you should believe or accept. It is intended to aid you in your own self-understanding. If you simply adopt what is said here as "the truth, the whole truth, and nothing but the truth," you block this learning process. No one can give you self-knowledge; you have to gain that yourself. What this book *can* do, if you read it with a critical mind and an open heart, is point you toward a deeper awareness. This in turn will lead to growth, change, and greater serenity and fulfillment in your life.

1

The Desire to Become

~

What would life be like if we did not need to be anybody other than who we are? What would happen if we had no concern about our image, about what other people think of us, about whether we measure up, or whether we're attractive enough, rich enough, or respectable enough? What if we were free to be who we are, what we are, at every moment? Imagine the joy and liberated energy that would be ours.

Chances are, such freedom escapes us. It eludes us because we're continually straining to become something better. We want to be happier, nicer, holier, more peaceful, more spiritual. We try to be self-actualized, successful, well-thought-of, more prominent, more powerful. This "desire to become" is the root of a good deal of unhappiness.

We also want our life to be different from what it is. We find that our job is boring, our boss is obnoxious, our spouse gets on our nerves. Our children aren't the way we want them to be. The world isn't right. Our life is not the way we think it should be. We're constantly struggling with the way things are, unhappy with the way life is. The result is that we are never at peace. We can never just be what we are, be with life as it is, because our minds endlessly chatter: "I'm not as I should be; life is not the way it should be."

Our desire for something different is the basis for the Christian notion of original sin. In Genesis 3:1-6, the account of the Fall, which gave rise to Christianity's teaching on original sin, Satan tempted the woman with the desire to become. He told her, "You will be like God." The woman took the fruit because it was "to be desired to make one wise." This desire was the temptation to be more than she was. With it, human misery entered the world.

The desire to be more, better, different, is the primordial sin, the original sin. All of us seem to struggle with this from the earliest years of our lives. In childhood we soon discover that love seems conditional: We're "good" if we behave properly, but "bad" if we don't. In school we try to be popular, acceptable, high achievers at academics or sports; our personal worth depends on it.

By the time we reach adulthood, the desire to become is a crushing weight upon us. We not only struggle for things like success and prestige, but we also seek to change all kinds of other things within ourselves. When we are angry, we want to be not angry. When we are afraid, we want to rid ourselves of fear. If we are insecure, we search for security and certainty in our life. If we admire someone else, we try to imitate that person. We strive to live up to the ideals of goodness and kindness that we learned when we were young. We continually strain to be more, better, different.

The modern plight resembles a sad-looking man who's in a tavern, slouched at the bar, drowning his sorrows in booze. The bartender says to him, "What's the trouble, Mack? Things can't be all that bad."

"Oh, yes, they are," the man says. "All my life, people have told me there's something wrong with me. My parents told me, 'The problem with you is that you're not quite what we wanted.' My teachers told me, 'You're not smart enough.' Women tell me, 'What's wrong with you is that you're boring.' My boss tells me, 'You're not productive.' And the Church tells me, 'What's wrong with you is that you're a sinner.' "

"You know," says the bartender, "you really should see a psychiatrist about this."

"I did," answers the man.

"Well, what did the psychiatrist say?" the bartender asks.

"Oh, he was just like all the rest!" the man cries. "He said, 'The problem with you is that you have a bad self-image.' "

We're forever trying to "fix" ourselves. There's always something about us that we feel we need to correct. This endeavor is the cause of so much unhappiness, and as we'll discuss later, the basis for fear, greed, and violence.

We might object, "Well, if I'm arrogant, egotistical, insecure, or rude, am I just to accept it and do nothing? That would simply give these things free rein in my life." The answer is that only when we can *be with* our fear, arrogance, or insecurity, does real change take place within us.

Suppose, for example, that I'm paralyzed by the fear of failure. I find it hard to do anything creative or risky because I'm afraid of messing up. To be free of my fear, I must understand it, but I can't understand it if I'm fighting it. If I resolve to become fearless, I'll end up battling my fear, struggling to overcome it. This prevents insight.

It is awareness, not our effort to become, that enables us to change. Let's watch our own need to become. Let's see how it hampers our self-understanding. As long as we are trying to control our fear, hide it, suppress it, stamp it out of our life, we will never gain the wisdom we need to let go of it.

To try to change ourselves just creates inner turmoil. Only when we can be fully who we are, fully with all that each of us recognizes as "me," can we begin to really change. This "being with what is" requires that we don't judge what we see in ourselves. Our desire to be different from what we are is the main obstacle here. It gives rise to constant judging of what we see in ourselves—and the ensuing need to fix what we see.

When we can be with what is, we can find peace, joy, even bliss, in our everyday lives. The trouble is that we are perpetually struggling with what's actually occurring in our lives. "I am stupid and foolish, and I should not be." "My spouse has faults that irritate me, so I distance myself from him." "My job is tedious, so I daydream about doing something else." Adam and Eve in the garden of Eden seem to have felt the same way. They lived in a state of primitive bliss, yet they wanted something different. That desire made them miserable.

In response to the Pharisees, who asked when the Kingdom of God would arrive, Jesus replied, "The kingdom of God is among you" (Luke 17:21). Instead of counseling us to wait for the Kingdom, Jesus said, "The time is fulfilled, and the kingdom of God has come near" (Mark 1:15).

We can live our entire life—indeed, go to our grave—deadened by the thought, "Things are not as they should be. My marriage, my job, my life, this world, isn't quite right. So I'll withhold my full attention and interest until things are as they should be." But the Christian response is that the Kingdom is here, that happiness is to be found here and now. "All the way to heaven is heaven," said Saint Catherine of Siena.[1] We need to surrender to the happiness that is found in being with what is.

"God saw everything that he had made, and indeed, it was very good" (Genesis 1:31). Life is a miracle, like a beautiful mountain vista. At first sight, the beauty of the vista takes our breath away, and we simply look at it in speechless wonder. But then we begin to say to ourselves, "This isn't quite as beautiful as the view I had yesterday, so I'm going to look elsewhere" or "I have too many problems and worries to spend my time looking at this, so I'm moving on." The consequence is that we are no longer with reality. We are with our chattering mind, in our own little world.

Mystics are those who have largely dropped the desire to become, and who are able to be with life as it is. John of the Cross put it succinctly when he wrote,

> To arrive at being all,
> desire to be nothing.[2]

The goal of the spiritual life is to discover that there is in fact no goal, that we are to be "that which, in God, we have always been," in the words of Meister Eckhart.[3] As Thomas Merton once said at an Asian conference of Christian and non-Christian monks, "My dear brothers, we are already one. But we imagine that we are not. What we have to recover is our original unity. What we have to be is what we are."[4] When we're no longer trying to become somebody, when we've ceased struggling to be anything, we are able to rest in the truth of what we already are.

The mystic path is about letting go of the conflict between ourselves and what is. When we're not preoccupied with how life should be different from the way it is, our minds can be quiet. We can perceive reality directly, without opinions or judgments clouding our vision. We can experience our unity with all creation and with a transcendent Presence at the heart of reality.

This is not an experience reserved for a select few. It's a possibility for all of us. It requires that we be present to what's happening at each moment of our lives. It means being completely absorbed with whatever it is we're doing, whether cooking a meal, mowing the lawn, taking a walk, or listening to someone who's talking to us. To do that is to live without any regrets from the past or worries about the future. This is true joy—a joy that naturally arises whenever we stop resisting what is.

It's not a matter of seeking enlightenment, spiritual highs, or a feeling of oneness with creation, although such experiences can occur. What's most important is that we live each moment in awareness. Enlightenment is a by-product of present-moment living; however, if we make it a goal, we remove our attention from the present. It becomes another excuse to believe that this moment is not as it should be, another reason to think that some future time, when we're enlightened, will be more worthy of our attention than what's occurring right now.

Our spiritual vocation involves giving up our resistance to the here and now. Needless to say, this is no easy task. The roots of the desire to become lie deep within us, and won't come out without a great deal of conscientious awareness. It's a gradual process, and probably the work of a lifetime for all of us.

When we drop our need to become, we are no longer separated from what we see. We discover our oneness with whatever we observe, whether it be other people, the world, or even things that we see within ourselves. For example, let's say I work for a company where there is fierce competition among the employees. Everyone is trying to get ahead, to outdo one another. My desire to get ahead, to be a success, separates me from my fellow employees. I see my co-workers not as they are but as threats to my own success. Only if I drop my desire to become can I perceive my oneness with other human beings, which is the reality.

If I view nature as something to be abused and exploited, I will never be able to be with nature as it is, to perceive its incredible beauty. If I see myself as stupid, or foolish, or cruel, and I react by condemning or trying to overcome those things within me, I create strife within myself. I will never gain the understanding I need to let go of my foolishness, because I'm too preoccupied with fighting it.

The essence of sin is separation: from God, from others, and from our true selves. The origin of this rift is our incessant need to change ourselves, and indeed to change life itself. The thought "I am not as I should be" or "Life is not as it should be" is the cause of all of our problems.

Some people have commented to me, "I think that we get a lot of energy from trying to improve ourselves. If I'm not trying to better myself, how will I ever have the motivation to do anything?"

We were born with extraordinary passion and energy. As infants, we had unbounded curiosity and spontaneity. Where did it all go? It's been suppressed by the overwhelming demand to be a good boy or a good girl, to live up to the expectations that parents, teachers, peers, and superiors have placed on us. The result is that we've lost the ability to be who we truly are. Someone criticizes us or hurts us, and we feel humiliated. And so, to protect ourselves, we withdraw a bit. After that, every time we're hurt, we withdraw a bit more. We have less and less energy because we're afraid of being hurt again, afraid of not being liked or approved of by others. It's no wonder that people have so little energy today. We've bought into the conformance game, and we've all paid the price.

To give an example, suppose there's an opening for the position of vice president at the company where I work. Suppose I want that position. It's important that I be aware of *why* I want it. If I want the position because it will mean more wealth, more power, or a more prestigious image for me, I am afflicted with the need to become. That brings greed and fear into my life: greed to be more and fear of losing status. It's the cause of ulcers, stress, and worry.

On the other hand, if I see that the company is making a genuine contribution to the overall well-being of society, and that I have the skills to do a good job as vice president and that I would thoroughly enjoy doing that job—that's creative motivation. There's a great deal of passion and energy behind such motivation, but we only find it when we get beyond our desire to be somebody important.

You may be thinking that I seem to be saying that children shouldn't be required to conform. "Don't children need to be disciplined as they grow up?" you may wonder. "Don't they need rules and standards to abide by?"

We certainly need to teach children how *to behave* appropriately. But we should be careful never to teach them how they are *to be*. In the home, children need to have rules and standards of conduct to follow, but without internalizing them psychologically. For example, a rule for family meals could be: "If you cry and scream at the dinner table, you will be sent to your room until you can settle down. You are not allowed to disturb everyone else's meal." In enforcing this rule, parents should clearly understand that the rule has nothing to do with whether the child is "good" or "bad." It is simply a house rule that is appropriate for the family. It is a consequence the children will learn to accept if their behavior is out of line. But it is strictly a behavioral rule. The behavior, not the person, is the focus.

So much damage is done to children when they are encouraged psychologically to internalize standards and rules. "You made your bed today, Johnny; you're a good boy." "You didn't do your homework; you're bad." "You got an 'A' in class; what a good girl you are." When we give these messages, we are setting in motion the harmful process of striving to become somebody better. The child learns, "I can please Daddy if I behave like he wants." As these children grow into adults, they will quickly go after other "approved" goals for their life: success, status, image, and so on. They will fall right into the conformance trap that has sapped the life out of so many people today.

2

How Do We Change?

~

We probably have a pretty good idea about the kind of person we'd like to be, the person we think we *should* be. We feel we ought to be pushing ourselves to become that person. And we *do* push ourselves, at least some of the time.

We would do well at such times to recall the Greek myth of Sisyphus, which was later used by the French novelist Albert Camus to symbolize the human condition. Sisyphus was punished by Zeus for his trickery by being compelled to roll a stone to the top of a slope in Hades, only to have the stone roll down again each time just as Sisyphus got it to the top. When we try to become the ideal person, we create for ourselves a similar plight. Like Sisyphus with his rock, we shove ourselves uphill, hoping to make it to the top. The higher we go, however, the greater the fall we have to fear. Each fall brings guilt and sadness.

People tell us we can make it to the top if we keep exerting ourselves. We all seem to believe this. But have we ever noticed that no one has yet accomplished much with all of this pushing and shoving? Have we ever stopped to see the utter futility of this inner struggle?

Seeking to conform to ideals, however noble they may be, is simply another example of our destructive desire to be different from what we are.

"I should be kinder than I am." "She is a loving person, and I want to be like her." "I realize that I can be ruthless and cruel; this goes against the Christian ideals I've been taught. I must work to rid my life of these things."

All of this creates a debilitating struggle and an enervating conflict in our life. We become disjointed people. Our ideals wage war within us against whatever doesn't measure up to the ideal.

We use our ideals constantly to judge what we see in ourselves, to disapprove of whatever falls short of the ideal, to try to change what we see, control it, suppress it. This ongoing battle is the cause of a lot of fear. We fear what's so. We are afraid to face the truth about ourselves, frightened to acknowledge the actual, fearful of having other people discover what's really true about us because it falls so short of the ideal.

Our inner struggle is also the source of violence. An internal combat rages between what should be and what is. Instead of being with what is, we continually fight against it, attempting to resist it, reshape it, or get rid of it. Is it any wonder that our external world is violent? War, brutality, ruthless competition—these are simply outward expressions of our inner selves.[1]

There will be no peace on earth until we address this turmoil within. As the Zen monk Thich Nhat Hanh would say, we have to put an end to the war inside us. We might think we can rid the world of war by adopting the ideal of peace: "To help eliminate war from the planet, I'll become a peaceful person. I'll get rid of the violence within me." But this merely sets up a new ideal to push for, a new source of inner strife. It's simply another attempt to be more than we are. No real change can result from this striving, since it still involves the struggle between the way things are and the way they ought to be.

As American pacifist activist A.J. Muste put it, "There is no way to peace—peace is the way."

In order for change to take place, we have to let go of our ideals. Our reaction to this might be, "Live without ideals? That's crazy. That would lead to chaos, an end to what we hold to be right and true." To answer this objection, we must distinguish between ideals as goals and ideals as possibilities.

When an ideal becomes a goal for our life, we have set in motion the whole violent process of striving to be different from what we are. "I am not a kind person, but I will make myself kind." "The Scriptures say that I should love my neighbor; therefore I will strive very hard to become loving." The battle between ideals and reality is merely intensified. The result is that we will now attack whatever we see within us that is not kind in our quest to reach the ideal. We will seek to become loving by being intolerant of all that is not loving within us. The contradiction here is obvious: Our first step in our attempt to become loving is intolerance and hatred of what's actually true about us. This crazy process is like building our house on sand: The wind and rain will come and destroy all our efforts.

A few years ago, an elderly person came up to me to complain, "For as far back as I can remember, I've had an uncontrollable tendency to gossip about people. I've tried and tried to stop it, to live without gossiping. Sometimes things seem to get better for a while, but eventually my gossiping returns,

maybe even worse than before." Any of us who have genu-
inely struggled with addictions, hurtful habits, or harmful ten-
dencies know this to be true: Willpower, efforts to conform to
the ideal, do not produce lasting change. If we are to drop our
hurtful tendency, we must be able to see it entirely as it is, to
discover the insecurity that gives rise to our need to gossip, to
see profoundly how our gossip harms us as much as it harms
those whom we gossip about. This requires we not judge the
gossip tendency, that we not try to achieve the ideal as a goal.

When an ideal is held as a possibility, instead of a goal,
then there is freedom really to see and understand what's actually occurring in our life. "I see that love, compassion, kindness, are beautiful things. These may be possibilities for my
life. However, I also see that striving to achieve them is a
futile process. Therefore, I will set them aside for the time
being. I will not attempt to become these ideals. Instead, I
will look deeply at what's actually happening in my life: my
egotism, my greed, my pettiness, and so on. I want to understand these things, to see how they arise, to see them deeply
without judging them." This kind of self-understanding leads
to true change.

When I was in my early twenties, I had a severe, daily dependence on alcohol that lasted for several years. I made what
I felt were herculean efforts to stop, but to no avail. My drinking actually increased. I experienced all the shame and self-
hatred that came from my conviction that "I shouldn't be
this way, I shouldn't have this weakness." Shame only made
the problem worse. I began to despair of ever being free of
this addiction. After a time, however, I saw the deep fear that
gave rise to my drinking and how I was allowing this insecurity to do real damage to my life. I cannot pinpoint exactly
when I had this insight. It was a moment beyond reasoning, a
moment when I was simply able to see my drinking habit

totally as it was. At that moment, I dropped my need to drink. It was only later that I realized, "I haven't wanted to drink for quite a while, and now that I think about it, that was a really destructive thing to do to myself. How could I have been so foolish?" Today, on occasion, I can consume moderate amounts of alcohol without a problem, since the addiction no longer exists. In general, however, I prefer not to drink. I find that even moderate amounts of alcohol cloud my awareness.

Haven't we all struggled to rid ourselves of an obnoxious behavioral tendency, but found that our efforts to change were to no avail? We may have become discouraged about ever attaining the change we wanted. Then, perhaps years later, we discovered that this hurtful habit no longer had power over us; we were free of it. We now noticed that we had a more detached view and a fuller understanding of the weakness and how it arose. We couldn't say when the change took place. In fact, the change took place without our reflecting on it, when we simply saw our habit thoroughly, as it was, and dropped it. In this way, we were taught an often overlooked truth: Change takes place through self-understanding, and this understanding is given to us when we can see ourselves as we are, without trying to change. "The Lord will fight our fight." We just need to be still, to be aware.

I think that it's possible for someone with an addiction—for example, alcoholism—to be completely free of it. But I don't think it's easy. Longstanding addictions and habits will not go away overnight. It may take years and years for us to gain the self-knowledge we need to get beyond the addictive compulsion. We sell ourselves short, however, by thinking, "I'll never be free of this. I'm a defective human being."

There are a number of good programs, such as Alcoholics Anonymous, available today to help people find a certain degree of healing from their addictions. A problem arises, however, when people become psychologically dependent on the program. Previously, they couldn't get through life without alcohol; now, they can't get through life without the program. They've simply substituted one dependence for another. This may be helpful for the short term, but as a long-term solution it's inadequate. It doesn't respect the full possibilities for healing and transformation that we human beings have. Some people, perhaps many, can one day be completely free of their addiction if they don't remain mired in this dependence.

Consider this analogy: If we are walking through a forest and suddenly come to a clearing where there is a steep and dangerous cliff, we immediately see the danger and step back. No deliberation, no inner struggle, are required. We instinctively stop before going over the precipice. In the same way, if we could fully see the danger of addiction, hurtful habits, greed, ruthlessness, we would drop those things right away. No inner debate would be necessary. The problem is that we can't notice the danger because our perception is clouded by our negative judgment of the addiction, our mindless efforts to fix our hurtful habit, our disapproval of the greed. These judgments and efforts only make us more preoccupied with the addiction. They serve only to make the habit worse by giving it more of our energy. We will always make such judgments as long as we hold ideals as goals to which we strive to conform.

Striving to become an ideal is simply a disguised form of self-interest. We want the ideal life for ourselves. We want what it will bring us. In preaching about this in my parish ministry, I try to help people see this by exposing the fear and debilitating guilt that surround our ideals.

We can fear those sides of ourselves that don't live up to the ideal: an addiction that threatens to ruin our life, an ugly behavioral weakness that we can't control. Why are we afraid?

We are anxious because we think we may lose the model life we so desire for ourselves. Or we're afraid that other people will disapprove of us if they should ever discover this weakness in us. Or we may be worried about how God will punish us, should this unseemly side ever take charge of our life. All of this fear and worry is self-interest. Our concern is: "What will happen to *me* if I transgress? What will God do to *me*? What will other people think of *me*?"

The same holds true with our guilt. Years ago, I was in a very competitive graduate studies program. The competition was so fierce that some of the students were tempted to cheat on exams. I remember hearing one student remark that the reason he would never cheat was because "I would just feel so guilty if I did." Apparently, his primary concern wasn't the effect his cheating might have on others in the program or how it might damage himself. He seemed mainly to want to avoid those unpleasant guilt feelings. I don't mean to single out that man. His candid remark points to something that can affect every one of us, without our realizing it. Ideals can easily foster a morality based on the avoidance of guilt. "How awful I would feel if I did that; I couldn't bear to feel that way." Again, this is simply self-interest.

I am not saying that self-interest is wrong or evil, but it is not love. As Saint Paul says, "[Love] does not seek its own interests" (1 Corinthians 13:5; *New American Bible* translation). Action based on self-interest is not love. The fear and guilt caused by ideals keep us in a childish state of immaturity, never able to move beyond self-preoccupation.

Love requires freedom, and freedom is impossible if we are motivated by fear or the avoidance of guilt. Surely, the Christian Church should be helping people to be liberated from these crippling motives. "Where the Spirit of the Lord is, there is freedom," said Saint Paul (2 Corinthians 3:17).

Ideals are both insidious and dangerous. Because of our deep-seated desire to be different from what we are, we hold almost every standard we have as a psychological goal. Each ideal becomes another reason to pretend that we're progressing up Sisyphus' mythical hill. It is very difficult to be aware of ideals as possibilities rather than goals.

Ideals as goals prevent us from seeing ourselves as we are. How many times in human history have so-called "Christian" nations waged war against neighbor nations, in the name of God or with the supposed approval of God? "If we are killing people, we are obviously justified in doing so because we are a Christian nation" is the thinking. Christian ideals easily blind us to our own brutality.

In our personal lives, our ideals can make us too ashamed to acknowledge responsibility for our hurtful actions. "I can't admit to that cruel thing I did. After all, I'm a nice person. Nice people don't do things like that."

A Catholic pastor whom I know said once, "When we identify ourselves with an ideal, we give up responsibility for everything we do that doesn't live up to that ideal. We don't deal with real evidence anymore. Our attitude is: 'Don't distort my dream with the facts.' " Once we've identified ourselves with a lofty standard, we lose touch with reality. We relinquish responsibility for facing the true facts about our life. In addition, as we have seen, ideals can quickly become a basis for making judgments about ourselves and others.

For much of its history, the Christian Church has seemingly taught its people to pursue Christian ideals as psychological goals. What has been the result? After two thousand years of Christianity, has human consciousness advanced to any appreciable degree? Are we any less violent today than people were two thousand years ago? Ruth Leger Sivard, in *World Military and Social Expenditures*, notes:

Beginning with the 17th century, every century has registered an increase in the number
of wars and in the number of deaths associ-
ated with them. The rise in war deaths has
far outstripped the rise in population. The
20th century in particular has been a stand-
out in the history of warfare. Wars are now
shockingly more destructive and deadly. So
far, in the 90 years of this century, there have
been over four times as many war deaths as
in the 400 years preceding.[2]

Clearly, we are not becoming less violent.

Are people any less fearful today than they were two thousand years ago? I think not, although we may be more subtle
and skilled at hiding our fear.

Many people today perceive a "crisis of authority" in the
Church and elsewhere. They are far less willing to listen to and
believe what those in authority tell them than previous gen-
erations. In the case of the Christian Church, this credibility
gap exists largely because the Church continues to speak from
the perspective of ideals, of what should be. In what some are
calling the "post-Christian era," people are beginning to realize
how futile and ineffective this perspective is and are searching for alternatives. Striving to conform to ideals does not
work. At best, it only makes for shallow or very limited change.
People are discovering this in their own lives and seeing this
confirmed in the lives of the Church's own ministers.

Ideals, however, are not just "the Church's problem." They
are our problem. What ideals are we pushing ourselves to
reach? With what result? Can we see the uselessness of it all?

"Judge not, lest you be judged," says Jesus. This scriptural
norm applies as much to the way we treat ourselves as to the

way we treat others. If we had no ideals, we would have no reason to judge or condemn others or ourselves. Awareness without judgment is the basis for freedom, love, and transformation.

"But," you many be thinking, "I'm not sure how Christ fits in with what you're saying. Aren't we supposed to try to be like Christ? Saint Paul said that we should imitate Christ. And shouldn't we be trying to be like the saints?"

Christians have traditionally held up the holy men and women of history as examples to emulate. And, yes, Saint Paul said, "Be imitators of me, as I am of Christ" (1 Corinthians 11:1). Also, we may have known men and women among our own families, friends, or acquaintances whose Christian faith was an inspiration to us.

Saints, holy men and women—these people have given us a powerful example of what life can be if it is lived in true selflessness. The difficulty is that Christians have sometimes seen the life of a holy person as something that they should try to copy.

Again, our childhood formation is crucial. From an early age we are told: Conform, imitate, follow the established script. We've brought this same approach into the Christian faith. To be like other holy Christians becomes a goal we should strive to attain. It's another form of the desire to become.

The effect is deadening. Not only have we set up a new ideal to pursue as a goal, with all the subtle self-seeking that goes with that, but we have taught people to live a second-hand life. Instead of living their own life in spontaneity and freedom, they have to try to imitate somebody else's life. It's a secondhand existence.

The German mystic Meister Eckhart taught that spirituality is a matter of subtraction, not addition.[3] True holiness, true emulation of holy people, involves our dropping the need to be somebody greater than we are. Instead of duplicating someone else's life, we can see the holy men and women of Christian history as possibilities whose lives may help to raise our awareness as to what may be possible in our own life.

What about Saint Paul's instruction that we imitate him as he imitates Christ? How are we to "imitate Christ"? I think that Paul gives us the answer to this question in what is perhaps his most powerful description of Christ:

> Let the same mind be in you that was in Christ Jesus, / who, though he was in the form of God, / did not regard equality with God / as something to be exploited, / but *emptied himself*, / taking the form of a slave, / being born in human likeness. (Philippians 2:5-8; emphasis added).

Jesus didn't try to become anybody important. In fact, he relinquished any such claim. He emptied himself. We imitate Jesus by our emptying of self, not by adding on ideals and standards, nor by trying to copy the lives of great people. To follow Christ is to abandon our desire to become.

3

Turnaround

~

U p until the sixteenth century, people generally
believed that all the planets in the solar system
revolved around the earth. The earth was the
center; *we* were the focal point of everything.

Then Copernicus, the Polish astronomer, discovered,
through careful observation of the planets, that the earth and
the other planets revolved around the sun.

This radical new theory about the earth and the planets
changed the whole perspective that people had about themselves and the world. We were no longer the center of the
cosmos.

In Matthew 3:1-6, John the Baptist challenges the people
of his day—and us—to make such a radical turnaround that
our whole perspective, our whole life, is changed. "The kingdom of heaven has come near.... 'Prepare the way of the Lord,
make his paths straight.' "

We can gain a deeper understanding of John's message by
rephrasing it: "The way you live right now, the way you think,
your whole perspective, is an *obstacle* to God's Kingdom," John

is saying. "If you don't want to be in the way, you're going to have to radically change how you look at life."

How might our perspective be an obstacle in God's way today? Let's look at the word "repent," as proclaimed by John the Baptist (Matthew 3:2). John the Baptist didn't speak English. He spoke a form of Hebrew (Aramaic). The word he used for repentance was probably *"tshuvah,"* a Hebrew word meaning a complete turnaround in life. "Look, people," John was saying, "you're moving in the wrong direction; turn around a hundred eighty degrees and make your way back toward God."

But then, in the fifth century, came Saint Jerome, who had the job of translating the Bible into Latin, the language of the day. *Tshuvah*[1] was a tough word to translate into Latin. The closest he could come was to use the phrase "do penance."[2]

When we try to translate John's words into English, we have similar difficulty. The closest we can come in English to the meaning of *tshuvah* is the word "repent." But "repent" is a tricky word; it means "to feel sorry." So, with our Latin and English translations, we understand John the Baptist's message as, "You've got to feel sorry, to do penance for the bad things you've done." But that's not what John was actually saying.

To a great extent, Christians still associate John the Baptist with the idea of shame, of feeling awful about who we are and the bad things we've done, beating our breast, making amends to get back in God's good graces. And it's precisely that perspective that is an obstacle to God's Kingdom, because it keeps us focused on ourselves.

Sometimes in my ministry, I encounter people who are obsessed with what they feel are some really rotten things about their life, some dark misdeed from the past, or some unseemly habit. And when I sense them dwelling on such things, I ask them, "Well, in all your guilt feelings, who is it that you're really focusing on; who is it that you're concerned about when you're tormented with this guilt?" Sometimes it's as if a light has been turned on for them, as they realize, "Why, it's myself; I'm dwelling on myself." And that's the point.

We can spend our whole life in the vicious circle of making a mistake, feeling guilty about it, then berating ourselves so as to get back in God's good graces, only to start the whole process all over again as soon as we make our next mistake. It's all so self-absorbed. And it's got very little to do with the Kingdom that John the Baptist was proclaiming.

Remember the gospel story about the miraculous catch of fish (Luke 5:1-11)? The apostles had been fishing all night and caught nothing. Jesus told them to cast their nets into the sea one more time. A skeptical Peter reluctantly agreed to do so. The disciples then caught such a great load of fish that their nets almost broke. It was a spectacular scene of God's power at work, but then Peter almost spoiled it. He blurted out, "Lord, I am a sinful man!" Jesus, however, paid little heed to Peter's anguish, and merely told him not to be afraid. It was as if Jesus was saying, "All right, Peter, you've had a lack of faith. It's okay. You're not the center of attention here. God's work is. So quietly acknowledge your lack of trust, learn from it, and then join the rest of us. You don't have to spoil the moment with endless self-concern."

In a real way, that is what John the Baptist's message is about: "Make ready for the One who is to come. You are not the center of attention. That belongs to the One who is to come." In other words, the Kingdom doesn't revolve around us, or around how we feel or think we should feel. The Kingdom is centered on God. We had better change our whole way of looking at things; we had better take ourselves out of the center of the meaning of "repentance"—otherwise we're just going to be in the way.

Barbara Taylor, a Christian preacher, puts it very well:

> Repentance has nothing to do with feeling sorry—about yourself or for yourself. Repentance is not a matter of listing all the things you wish you had not done in your life and feeling badly about them, as if you could dilute them somehow with your regrets. Repentance is not about wishing you were a better person or keeping track of your faults, as if God might be persuaded to overlook them if only you could convince him that you are really, really, really, really sorry....Repentance is not deciding to be nicer, or more generous, or more spiritual. It is not, for that matter, something that is under our control....
>
> Repentance is more something that happens to you than something you decide....Repentance is a complete turnaround, a change of course, a change of heart and mind and life. Repentance is too busy redeeming the present to apologize for the past. Repentance spends less time hating the bad than loving the good. Repentance is a matter of being grasped by God, of being picked up and put down again so that everything looks different, so that you lose your old bearings and are offered new ones instead. That is God's part in the process, anyhow. Our part is to have the good sense to say "thank you" instead of "no" or "not yet," and to learn

> how to steer by those new lights instead of
> scrambling to return to our old familiar
> ones...
>   It is not, I think, something that happens
> only once. Life is full of such turning points,
> both large and small...[3]

Repentance is being open to discovering that we are not the center of the universe; we're not even the center of our solar system.

Some people who have been diagnosed with a terminal illness say this: "Hey, I'm dying; not too long from now, I won't even be here. My life has been pretty shallow up till now. It's time to change, to really share my gifts, during the days I have left." That's repentance.

Or maybe we're suddenly called to take care of an elderly relative who's become an invalid; or there's a setback in our job or family life and we've got to give of ourselves more than we ever have before. That's an occasion for repentance.

Or, after years of struggling with an addiction and getting nowhere, we stop condemning it and begin to simply see how damaging this mindless behavior has been to ourselves and to others; then we decide that this is not how we want to live our life. And behold, the addiction starts to lose its grip on our life. That's repentance.

Repentance is about letting go of our endless preoccupation with "me."

For every one of us, to repent means to begin to notice all of those thought patterns and attitudes that keep life revolving around "me"—the guilt, the shame, the fear, including the fear of God—all of which cause us to stop the action of life, to hold back and to focus on ourselves. To become aware of all of those things and to begin to leave them behind is to repent.

It's truly a Copernican revolution to which John is calling us. It's such a change of heart and mind that the way we view life, the way we look at the world, is spun completely around. It's to discover that the center of everything is not this little self of mine, but this One Who Is Love.

4

The Really Good News

~

I n the ancient Near East, the people believed that when a king erected a temple to a god or to several gods, that temple building was a sign of the gods' permanent approval of the continuing rule of the king and his descendants.

In the second book of Samuel 7:1-11, we see King David, who has defeated all his enemies, peacefully settled in his palace. Like any wise king, he decides to build God a temple, because that way he and his people would be sure to remain in the good graces of God for a long time to come. God's care and protection would be secured forever.

But God, through the prophet Nathan, says to David, "Should *you* build *me* a house [temple] to dwell in? Look at all that I have done for you. I took you from your life as a sheepherder and made you king of an entire nation. No, I will build a house [dynasty] for you. You will be my people, my temple, forever."

David thought he had to do something to secure God's love, but in fact he already had what he sought. His relationship with God was secure already. He didn't have to do anything to ensure it. But that was extremely difficult for him to comprehend.

We humans have repeated David's mistake throughout history. In the fifth century, a man named Pelagius said that because we humans have such powerful free will, there is no height of sanctity that we cannot attain if we only have the courage to will it. "I can save myself, better myself, make myself holy, through my own willpower" was the thinking. The Christian Church condemned Pelagius' thinking as heretical, since it denied the necessity of God's grace. We do not *achieve* salvation; it is always God's gift to us.

The Pelagian heresy is alive and well today. Some call it the greatest heresy in the contemporary Church: the attitude that we earn our salvation. If we put forth the effort, attend church, do good works, and steer clear of sin, we will achieve the sanctity we deserve.

In a famous television commercial for a stock-brokerage firm, the narrator says, "We make money the old-fashioned way: We *earn* it." Often we Christians view holiness and salvation in the same way: We earn them, we achieve them. Or so we think. This is simply modern Pelagianism.

There is a story about a squatter who lived in a shack on some fertile land way out in the middle of nowhere. He was able to feed himself off the land, but he kept a low profile because he was never sure when the owner of the land might come and evict him.

One day the landowner did come. But he didn't evict the squatter. Instead, he said to him, "See those hills all the way over there, on the west and on the north horizon? You can have all the land from here to there. And the forest and the lake that are as far as you can see to the south and the east— all the land from here to there is yours, from horizon to horizon. All I ask is that you not abuse the land."

But the squatter had never experienced a gift like this before. He really couldn't understand it. The landowner's words were unbelievable. And so after the landowner departed, the squatter tried to follow the instructions he thought he had heard. "Well," he said to himself, "when he talked about my boundaries on the north and west, he was walking near this rock and that tree; and when he pointed out my boundaries on the south and east, he was standing by that stump and that boulder yonder. So my land is bounded by the rock, the tree, the stump, and that boulder."

And so the squatter fenced in about an acre of land, according to those limited boundaries. He spent months improving the fence, making it bigger and stronger, so as to keep out strangers. He built a house and a barn that he hoped would impress the landowner. He spent his remaining years maintaining and improving all that he had built, fearful that he might be evicted if he ever let up. Finally, in old age, the squatter died. He had worked hard to keep up his property, but he died without ever having realized or enjoyed the enormous gift he'd been given.

Like that man in the story, and like David in the book of Samuel, we can live our lives as if we are fenced-in, thinking we have to earn God's favor. This is especially true in our American culture, where one has to work to achieve anything important. A degree, a good job, the good life, even respect from other people—none of these things are free, it seems. We have to work hard, pay our dues, show that we're worthy of these rewards. There's no free lunch. If you don't have to earn it, it's not worth much.

And so, when it comes to something as important as salvation, shouldn't we have to earn that as well? We have to keep ourselves in God's good graces, build up those heavenly credits, so that we can attain our final reward.

All of this is just a mercenary mind-set, thinking that we can turn the gift of salvation into a reward, compensation for services rendered. It is lifeless, fenced-in behavior.

From the early days of its history, our Church has condemned the heresy that we can secure God's love by our efforts, that we earn God's favor. But it's a heresy that keeps creeping back to poison our life of faith.

God wants our hearts, not our sacrifice. God wants our love, not our mercenary behavior.

As Brother David Steindl-Rast, OSB, once said, "The bad news is that we can't make up for what we have done in the past. But the good news is that we don't have to."

Do we believe that? Does that upset us? It upset the people in Jesus' day. As a matter of fact, it probably got Jesus killed. Donald Senior, one of the most respected contemporary Catholic biblical scholars, writes about it this way:

> Jesus of Nazareth, then, had a special rapport with those on the margins [tax collectors, prostitutes, the unclean woman]: he befriended them; he apparently ate with them; and many of them seemed to join his following. Some recent studies of the historical Jesus have pointed to this as one of the most important causes of tension between Jesus and the religious leadership of his day. Certainly no Jew would object to sinners repenting and resuming their place in the community of Israel, so the offense of Jesus' ministry to those on the margin must have been something more. Could it have been, as some have speculated, that Jesus freely associated with sinners and had table fellowship with them

before requiring them to repent of their of-
fenses? Was this radical stance by a respected
religious leader in a time of reform what
caused scandal and hostility to mount against
Jesus? The Gospels indicate that this may well
be the case.[1]

In other words, Jesus became friends with all the worst sinners of the day. He spent a great deal of time with them. He
enjoyed meals with them. And it seems that he did all of that
without requiring that they change. Jesus' attitude toward these
sinners was: "You're fine the way you are; God respects you
utterly as you are; you don't have to change. Of course, if you
respected yourself as much as God does, you wouldn't allow
yourself to be abused, and you wouldn't stoop to abusing others. So don't change yourself; just know yourself; know God's
love, which is already the deepest part of you, and then you'll
realize on your own what you need to do about your lifestyle."

This attitude enraged the devout religious leaders of the
day. They felt they had worked hard, very hard, to merit God's
favor. How unthinkable that those who had never lifted a
finger for God should have the same reward. And so these
religious leaders concluded that Jesus had to be silenced. He
had to be killed.

Today, whenever we think that we have to change who we
are, or other people have to change who they are, in order be
acceptable, we too silence the good news.

5

The Courage to Search

~

In the ancient world, there was a belief among people of different religions that a universal king would come to the world. But most people believed this universal king would come from the East.

The Magi, who were astrologers, lived in the East. But they weren't so provincial as to think that this king would have to be found somewhere in their own backyard. They were more open-minded, more receptive, than that. And so, when they saw a star, a star that they believed to be a very important astrological sign, they pulled up stakes and followed it. They went west. They followed the star to parts unknown. They found the Christ child, and they believed. Truly extraordinary people, these Magi!

The story of the wise men is a powerful challenge to us. Their example shows us that Christ can frequently be revealed to us in new, different experiences. If we want to learn more about Christ, if we want to experience Christ more deeply in our lives, then we have to be open to things that might seem alien, threatening to us.

So often, perhaps, this is not the case for us. So often we can be comfortable with what we already know, satisfied with the things we understand—we feel we don't need to look at anything new. This may be especially true when it comes to our religious beliefs.

There's an old Sufi tale about a man who was out in a field, on his knees, searching for something. His friend came by and asked, "What are you looking for?" The man replied, "I'm looking for my key; I lost it." And so they both got down on their knees to look for the lost key. After they'd searched together for a while, the friend finally said, "Well, where did you lose this key?" The man replied, "I lost it on the other side of the road." The friend said, "Good heavens! Then why are you searching for it over here?" "Because," the man replied, "there is more light over here."

We can be a lot like that man. We look for Christ only where the light is. We stick to the familiar, preferring not to look into anything new.

I grew up in the pre-Vatican II Catholic Church. There was a real tendency then to feel that we Catholics had all the answers. All non-Catholics were labeled "unbelievers," and we questioned seriously whether anybody could be saved if they weren't Catholic.

And then the Church did something difficult; it convened a council to reexamine some of the old beliefs and stereotypes. The Church in the Second Vatican Council said some things that sounded new. One of the things the Council said was that the Kingdom includes even those people who aren't Christian. Jews, Hindus, Buddhists, Muslims—they're all part of the Kingdom. Truth can be found in these non-Christian religions, the Church said.

Are we receptive to hearing that truth? Are we open to

listening to what these other religions might be able to tell us? If we are, we can learn more about Christ.

The Jesuit scholar William Johnston has said that by the next century the Eastern religions—for example, Buddhism—will have had a profound impact on Christianity. A positive impact. Are we receptive to this?

My own prayer life has been strongly influenced by Zen Buddhism. I have found that Zen meditation can be a profound form of contemplative prayer, a prayer of silence. It is a prayer that helps one to live more fully in each present moment of every day, to find God's presence in every moment. In my earlier years, I would never have thought that I could learn anything valuable from Buddhism. We already have the truth; what can they teach us? was my attitude. But I have to thank the East for this method of prayer, and the Christian "magi" who helped bring it to us—people like Thomas Merton, Anthony de Mello, Ruben Habito, and others.

When we begin to investigate something that seems foreign to us, especially when it's a basic thing like religion or spirituality, we're uncomfortable because we no longer feel safe. A new experience may cause us to have doubts about our once-secure convictions, and we feel threatened by that. But the doubt is important. If we don't hide from the doubt, if we face it and work through it, it can lead us closer to Christ.

In my seminary days, I was blessed to have a very fine theological education. I studied under some of the best scholars in our Church. I remember, in the midst of my studies, feeling utterly certain of my faith. I felt that it all made sense. One summer, during a break from my studies, I spent a number of weeks studying Spanish in Spain. While in Spain, I met a man in his late twenties who was originally from Germany. He was a very intelligent man, well educated and fluent in several languages. One day he and I had a conversation about faith. He told me that he was an atheist, pure and simple. "God doesn't exist," he said. "God is a figment of our imagination. People created the idea of God to make up for the pain, the loneliness, the despair, of their lives," he continued. I tried to respond by talking about my experience of a loving God, but this man would hear none of it. "If such a loving God exists," he demanded, "then why is there so much evil, so much suffering, tragedy, and death in the world; how could all of this be if a loving God exists?"

I was very uncomfortable with that conversation. What that man said really disturbed me. His doubts, his questions, cut right to the heart of my faith. For the next several years, I searched for answers to his questions. I studied, I prayed, I asked questions of scholars and faith-filled people. In the end, I came upon some interesting theories, but no conclusive answers as to why evil can exist in a world created by a loving God: There are no conclusive answers to that question. What was far more important for me, however, was the effect that this whole questioning process had on my life. It changed me. It helped me to see that faith involves not just belief, but a willingness to live with what cannot be known, a surrender to a Presence that can never be understood. Those questions led me closer to God. And so, today, I am grateful for that talk with the German atheist.

Doubt is the friend of faith, not a threatening darkness from which we need to shy away. Think about your own faith: Do you have questions? Things that you're not so sure you believe? Things that you might call into question if you really looked into them? Don't suppress those questions. The example of the wise men challenges us not to fear those doubts. They can actually strengthen our faith if we confront them and try to work through them.

The story of the Magi who left home and went searching

for God in an alien land tells us that Christ can be more deeply revealed to us through experiences that might seem new, foreign, threatening. If we are willing to leave the familiar, to venture forth from the light and into the darkness, we can come ever so much closer to Christ.

6

Self-Awareness

~

"You are my Son, the Beloved; with you I am well pleased" (Mark 1:11). These words of total love, acceptance, and mission are meant for Jesus as he is baptized by John in the Jordan. It's important to remember that the man Jesus hadn't yet done anything to merit these words. He hadn't yet withstood Satan's temptations in the desert. He hadn't healed any sick, or given sight to any of the blind. He hadn't proclaimed a word about the Kingdom. He hadn't yet been obedient unto death. Jesus heard this voice not because of anything that he had done, but because his mind was awake and his heart was fully open.

Through our baptism, these same words are spoken to each of us. "I have called you friends, because I have made known to you everything that I have heard from my Father" (John 15:15), Jesus said. And he prayed "… that the world may know that you [Father] have sent me and have loved them even as you have loved me" (John 17:23). The same Spirit of divine acceptance that came over Jesus descends upon us in our baptism. God is well pleased with us, as we are. God's favor rests upon us, right now—we don't have to wait for it. An experience of ultimate belonging is offered us, if we are open to it. We don't have to be anybody other than who we really are in order to have it.

But to a great extent, the way we live our lives denies the truth of our baptism. We don't think we measure up, and so we spend our life trying to measure up, attempting to improve ourselves, striving to make ourselves better than what we are. We only harm ourselves, and often others as well, in the process.

Imagine a newly married couple who have had their first big argument. Part of the dispute arose because the wife was irritated by something that the husband did. After the argument, the husband is depressed. He goes to see a marriage counselor to talk about the matter. The husband says to the counselor: "I don't want to have any more troubles like this in my marriage. I don't want any more arguments. I'm going to change who I am in order to please my spouse."

Any competent counselor, and probably all of us, could see how futile and even ridiculous the husband's plan is. The husband can't change who he is—not really. Oh, he can use all kinds of willpower to fake it for a while, to put on a nice, agreeable facade in order to keep peace in the marriage. But his efforts will only make for a superficial, if not a miserable, marriage relationship. He would be far better off if he would simply look at his attitudes and behavior patterns that are contributing to the trouble in the marriage. Through coming to an awareness, he can begin to let go of these hurtful attitudes. However, he can never change who he really is, and he does violence to himself by thinking that he can.

The same is true in our relationship with God. We think we have to change who we are in order to measure up, to please God. Our first mistake is thinking that we can change who we are. Like the deluded husband, we can't; such thinking only does violence to ourselves. Our second mistake is thinking that we have to please God. We don't. God is already pleased with us. After all, God created us. How could God not be pleased with who we really are? That's the good news of our baptism.

There's an old saying, "God doesn't make junk." The trouble is that we don't see that, we don't believe it. We think we need to repair ourselves, improve who we are. And so we're terribly concerned about the impression we make; we're worried about how other people perceive us. We want others to be pleased with us, or to appreciate us more. We're anxious about whether we're as successful or as prosperous as we should be. We want to be more important, more prominent, more admired. We even try to impress God (as if we could!) by trying to make ourselves holier, kinder, better.

Think of the price we pay for all of this attempted self-improvement: the tremendous waste of energy, the distress, the worry, the ulcers, the depression, the fear, the unhappiness. It's all a violent process, violent to ourselves, violent to our children, violent to our world community. It only leads to misery and sadness. It's a dead-end street.

Our baptism tells us that the real me, the real you, doesn't need fixing or changing. We don't need to improve ourselves. We just need to be aware.

To try to change what I am is to remain in prison. Let's say that I'm self-centered and judgmental. I notice that I associate only with people who like me, and that I frequently say bad things about people whom I don't like. I find that I am living in a prison cell of my own judgmentalism. So I tell myself that I am no longer going to be that way. From now on, I will try not to be so unkind. Trying not to be unkind is like redecorating the dreary walls of my prison cell with pretty pictures. My cell looks nicer now, I've put up a more pleasant covering, but I'm still in prison. I'm not free.

We may think, "I shouldn't be spiteful, I shouldn't do unkind things, I shouldn't gossip." Of course we shouldn't do those things. But trying to be a person who doesn't gossip only increases our inner struggle; it only strengthens the bars of that prison cell that encloses us.

We break out of prison when we see that we don't have to fix ourselves: We only have to understand the anger and the insecurity that give rise to things like gossip.

Instead of trying to get rid of our anger, we can watch it. This is truly a discipline of awareness: every day, to watch all the ways we become angry, irritated, frustrated; to watch all of that, experience it. We can then begin to see the fear that underlies our anger, and how big a factor fear is in our lives. We can be with the fear and the anger whenever they arise, without judging them or trying to rid ourselves of them. Out of that discipline of awareness comes growing understanding, and with understanding we begin to be free of fear, anger, self-centeredness.

The problem is that we don't want to notice our anger. We'd rather pretend that we're kind and loving people. It feels better to identify ourselves with some ideal. It's hard to be aware of what's actually true about our life. Often we don't like what we see in ourselves. We'd rather spend our time making our prison cell look nicer by putting all those ideals on the walls.

To be aware is to live the reality of our baptism: that we don't have to redo ourselves, we don't have to correct who we are in order to find God. We just need to be awake.

There's a story about a little fish who wanted to find the ocean. The fish swam around asking all the older fish, "Where is this thing they call the ocean?" One older fish told him, "If you do good deeds, and try very, very hard to be a good fish, then one day you will find the ocean." Finally, the little fish swam to the oldest, wisest fish in the whole sea, and asked him, "How can I find the ocean?" And the wise old fish just laughed.[1]

We think we have to try to be good in order to find the Kingdom, but the Kingdom is already here, in our midst (Luke 17:21). We feel that we have to please God, but our Creator God is already pleased with us. We work to obtain God's favor, but we're already embraced by that divine favor. We don't need to secure any of these things. They've already been given to us. All we need to do is wake up.

7

What's Our Motivation?

~

Our well-being is a valid concern, but what's our motivation? A few years ago in one of the western states, there was an uproar about pesticides that landowners were spraying on some of their crops. Some of these pesticides proved to be toxic to humans who came into contact with them. Whole families were working in the fields, and sometimes several members of the family, even the children, would become ill. A government inspection team began to investigate the effects of the pesticides. The team wanted to interview several families who had been hit by illness. But the parents were reluctant to be interviewed, even though their children had become sick. They said, "Don't use our names, don't quote us, because we could lose our jobs." Their children were being poisoned, but their fear of losing their jobs outweighed that consideration.

It's only proper to be concerned about our job, our material needs: but what's our motivation? Do we perform our job just for the money, even though it's damaging our health, hurting us, hurting our family? Are we doing a legitimate thing for the wrong reason?

In Luke 4:1-13, the devil tempted Jesus with what appeared to be legitimate concerns. Jesus had eaten nothing for many days. He was famished. So the devil urged him, "Turn this stone into bread and feed yourself."

Then the devil showed Jesus all the earthly kingdoms. He told Jesus, "Look, you're the Messiah. You deserve to have power over the whole world. Just do what I ask, and you'll get what's rightfully yours."

Finally, the devil set Jesus on the parapet of the temple in Jerusalem, tempting him to seek the status he deserved: "People don't realize how special, how important, you are. So throw yourself down from these temple heights, and your angels will save you in a spectacular way. And then everybody will be so impressed that you'll get the recognition you deserve."

These were not evil things in themselves: food, the important role Jesus was supposed to have, the recognition the Son of God ought to have. But the motivation behind them *was* harmful. The devil tempted Jesus to amass all the power and recognition for himself, to rely on himself alone, instead of his Father, for guidance and sustenance.

In his play *Murder in the Cathedral*, T.S. Eliot tells the story of Saint Thomas à Becket. Thomas à Becket had resigned as chancellor when he became archbishop of Canterbury. He realized the danger of corruption involved in holding the position of archbishop while still under the authority of the king. The king, however, was greatly displeased, because he wanted Thomas to hold both positions at once. But Thomas refused to give in to the king's demand. At one point in the play, Thomas is returning to England, where he knows the king will have him put to death. During this trip, the devil presents Thomas with three major temptations: the temptation to protect his own physical well-being by giving in to the king's demand; the temptation to seek the power involved in being both chancellor and archbishop; and the temptation to preserve the friendships he will lose if he persists in his path toward martyrdom. Thomas easily avoids all three of these temptations. But then the devil offers him the clincher, the fourth and greatest temptation: to go ahead and be martyred, because that way Thomas will become a great saint. "People will flock to your tomb, seeking miracles," the devil tells him. It's the temptation of spiritual greed.

Thomas à Becket is on the verge of martyrdom, sainthood, yet this spiritual temptation shakes him to the core. Thomas knows that to be faithful to his convictions, even unto death, is the right thing to do. But wouldn't it be great to do the right thing and gain spiritual renown in the process? What could be so wrong with that? It is only with the greatest difficulty that he doesn't succumb to this temptation. In sidestepping this enticing lure, he says, "This then is the greatest treason: to do the right thing for the wrong reason."

The call to conversion in the passage from Luke's Gospel is the very same: Are we doing seemingly laudable things for the wrong reason?

I once knew a man who was a geologist. He loved being a geologist. He loved to be out in the dirt, the rocks and the muck, digging, cutting up rocks, looking at rock formations. And because he was so good at what he did, he was offered a promotion to supervisor. He accepted the new position, but he then spent all his time in the office. He became miserable because he was no longer in the field. When someone asked him why he took the promotion to supervisor, he replied, "Well, it will look good on my résumé. It's important to have a good résumé if you are going to move up."

Is our career advancement making us or our family un-happy? What's our motivation? Do we pursue recognition as a goal for what we do? The friends I have, the kids I hang around with at school—do I associate with these people be-cause they are important or popular, so that I look good as a result? The sports I'm involved in or the grades I earn or the achievements I make—am I just doing it to be recognized?

It can be a real eyeopener to see how much of what we do can be governed by our need to look good: the jobs we take, the clothes we wear, the homes we buy, the things we say and do. How much is my need to look good directing all of this?

We can ask the same questions about our virtues, our good qualities. Suppose I think that humility is the highest virtue. And so I work at being humble. I try never to be the center of attention, never to talk too much. I always keep a low profile. I do everything I can to live up to some image I have about humility. Why do I do this? My attempt to achieve humility is in fact just a subtle way to look good to God, or to others, or even to myself. It's a clever way to impress. Think about that. Conscious humility is a subtle form of arrogance. It's self-seeking. Such is always the case when we seek to achieve a virtue as a goal—it becomes *my* goal, *my* achievement. On the other hand, true virtues like love and humility rise to the surface as a natural part of our life when we're no longer think-ing about self-advancement but just doing what needs to be done in the present moment.

Why am I a Christian? Why do I attend church? Do I do so out of fear? Am I afraid of the punishment I feel I will receive if I don't? Do I help my neighbor because I fear God's wrath? Fear is self-interest: I'm worried about what will happen to me if I don't help my neighbor. Do I do good deeds in order to earn my heavenly reward? Seeking a reward is self-concern.

Christianity is not just another means to further our self-interest. If it were, we might as well close and lock the church doors forever, because the world offers quicker and more gratifying ways to satisfy the demands of the self than we do. Christianity is, rather, a call to forget about the self, to move beyond self-interest as the motivation for what we do.

The good news is that, like the shepherd who abandons everything to seek out the lost sheep, God needs almost no excuse to welcome us into the fold. God accepts us, gathers us in, even though we're motivated by self. But God offers us a far more fulfilling life than the dead-end street of self-seeking. God offers us freedom from fear, and the happiness that comes from self-forgetting.

The devil presented Jesus with three powerful temptations—powerful because they all dealt with legitimate concerns. But Jesus, fully open to the Spirit, was aware of Satan's trap. He saw the blatant self-interest behind each temptation. His awareness enabled him to be free of self. Awareness can free us too.

We need only allow the Spirit to enlighten us, to help us see why we really do the things we do—however praiseworthy they may seem to be on the surface. Then we will have within us the liberating grace of awareness.

8

Transforming Our Vision

~

Our faith tells us that there is more to reality than the physical things we see every day—that there is an invisible world of the holy that permeates our visible world. Sometimes the veil is lifted; the curtain that hides the Infinite is drawn back, and we experience directly the splendor and the mystery that normally seem hidden.

The Transfiguration (Mark 9:2-10) was such a moment. Jesus took Peter, James, and John to the mountaintop, where he was transformed before their eyes. His clothes became dazzlingly white. Jesus was revealed as who he truly was: the exalted, glorious Lord.

The disciples were rendered speechless by this experience. "They were overcome with awe," the gospel says. Peter tried to make some sense out of the situation by offering to build three booths at the site. But the event remained beyond the disciples' ability to comprehend.

The Transfiguration brought home to the disciples, and it can bring home to us, that life is more than just humdrum routine. Reality is filled with God's magnificence. What's more, we don't have to have a mountaintop experience to know this. In fact, we have to accompany Jesus and the disciples down from the mountain. It's in our everyday lives that the miraculous is to be found.

But the truth is that we can largely miss the splendor of God in our everyday lives. Life can be tedious, draining; it can even seem meaningless. Why is this? The main reason, the mystics tell us, is that we look at the world as an object. Everything we see we view in terms of the fulfillment of our needs: "Can this thing give me what I want or need? If not, I'm not interested in it." When we see another person, we react, at least unconsciously, with thoughts like, "Will this person be pleasing or helpful to me? Is this person a threat or a pain to me?" We're attracted to or repelled by other people on the basis of this constant inner chatter. Other people become blips on our radar screen: "Are they friend or foe?" we ask. Reality as a whole becomes something that we try to use and shape, and even avoid, to fit our needs.

The result is that we don't see people or things as they are. We see them as objects of our needs and wants. We miss the miraculous that is at the heart of everything.

I know a couple who bought a home on a beautiful stretch of land, in an area where the sunsets are frequently spectacular. They spent years improving their property: clearing the field behind the house, putting up a fence, building a deck, and so forth. All their free time went into this work. But, as they told me later, they never noticed the sunsets until several years after they had bought the property, when a friend visited them one evening and pointed out a particularly gorgeous sunset.

Isn't that the way we tend to live? I include myself in this generalization, because I struggle with this. Our minds are swimming with our plans, our concerns, our worries, and our wants. We constantly judge, analyze, and evaluate things in terms of their usefulness to us. We don't see things as they really are. We don't perceive the world as it actually is.

If we look deeper, we'll probably find that we can treat God as an object too. Ask yourself, "What comes to mind when I think of God?" A white-bearded man in the sky who keeps tabs on my transgressions? Someone who will rescue me whenever I'm in trouble? Almost any time we think of God, we make God into an object—someone or something "out there," apart from us, who threatens us, punishes us, pleases us, or fills our needs. We so easily see God only in terms of our wants. We don't relate to God as God is.

The scene cited from the Gospel of Mark comes shortly after Peter's great confession that Jesus was the Messiah, the Anointed One of God (Mark 8:29). For many people today, Peter's statement would not have much appeal. Why is this? Why do some call this the "post-Christian era"? Why are many Christian denominations losing members today? This is a complex issue, but a major part of the answer lies in the fact that Christianity has made God into an object. Too many Christians can regard God as a stern parent whom we have to try to impress so that he'll give us our heavenly reward. Or God is a warm-fuzzy figure who asks us to be nice. What kind of God is that? Not a very credible one. A God who is an object has less and less appeal for people these days. It's no wonder that many of the Christian churches are losing members.

If we Christians are to be the Body of Christ, if we are to be God's light to the world, then we had better be worshiping the true God, the exalted Lord whose presence is so tangible to us, so awesome, that we're at a loss for words. That's a God whom people can devote their lives to.

So how do we enter into relationship with such a God? How can we live in today's world without turning everything into an object? Consider the personal account of Philip St. Romain, a husband, a father, and a Christian. After years of being faithful to a practice of contemplative prayer, he underwent an enormous transformation. He speaks about it this way:

> Before [the transformation]...my awareness seemed to be housed in the intellect. No matter how hard I tried, I could not "just look" or "just be" without thinking, analyzing, and judging what I was perceiving. Consequently, I was always one thought away from perfect silence—and I knew it....[Now], however, it seems that my awareness breaks free from the intellect and so is able simply to experience reality through the sense without judging, analyzing or thinking. It becomes possible to just-look, and to see things as they are without distorting them through an interpretive filter. Sitting and looking at a leaf, or a tree, listening to a bird becomes a powerful religious experience; it is as though I am seeing everything for the first time....On one level, nothing is different; everything still has its familiar shapes, colors, smells, sounds, etc. And yet there is no denying the fact that everything seems new, special—a center of God's presence. This latter perception is a contribution of faith to this seeing, opening my heart to the fact that God is the center of everything. Intellectually, I always knew this; now I can see that it is true.[1]

Philip St. Romain credits the practice of a prayer of silence as helping to prepare him for the gift of this new awareness.

The gospel also speaks of the need for preparation. The Transfiguration account says that it was "after six days" that Jesus took Peter, James, and John to the mountaintop (Mark 9:2). Six days was the traditional length of time required for preparation and self-purification before one could have a close approach to God.[2] In other words, the disciples were able to witness the glorious Transfiguration because they were ready for it, having been through the traditional period of purification. Their minds were clear and attentive. We too need a practice of preparation and attentiveness to sense the miraculous in our everyday world.

During the Lenten season, for example, it's important to limit, or even eliminate altogether, the time we spend watching television. So much of what is aired on television is numbing amusement. It can be a heavy contributor to a mindless existence. Turn off the television and the video games, at least for a certain period of every day; shut off the stereo, and allow yourself to encounter reality.

Whatever you do in your daily life, try to do it mindfully. Feel your shoes against the pavement as you walk down the street. Smell the clean clothes as you take them out of the dryer. Sense the wind against your face. Observe your distracting thoughts and worries as they arise.

It's also important to have some practice of silent prayer in our daily lives. We have to find a way to pray in which we don't make God into an object of our wants. Breathing Prayer and Centering Prayer are two possibilities. (See Appendix II.) A true prayer of silence is one that allows us to quiet our inner chatter and surrender ourselves to the God who is ultimately beyond our capacity to comprehend. Do we have some way of praying that enables us to surrender, a prayer where our focus is not "my will" but "your will be done"? This kind of prayer opens us to the Real.

When we're silent, just experiencing reality, God can transform us. For most of us, this process takes place slowly. Over a period of months and years, a regular practice of silent prayer progressively heals us of our need to see everything as an object. We begin to sense something wondrous in the midst of our familiar world. We discover a Reality that can render us speechless.

The Transfiguration isn't something that happened only to Jesus; it's an event that he wants to share with all of us. Our lives are to be transformed too. We are transfigured when we sense the miraculous in the ordinary, when we experience God's wondrous presence in our daily lives. We don't have to go to a mountaintop for this to happen. We can open ourselves to it now, wherever our life is. We just have to be attentive, to be willing to see things as they really are.

9

Healing Our
Source Relationship

~

The Fourth Commandment tells us to "honor your father and your mother," but what does this mean? Of course it includes obeying our parents while we are growing up; caring for them in their old age; respecting them throughout our life. Those things are important. But it's more than that.

The Commandment says that our parents are to be honored in order "that your [their children's] days may be long in the land that the Lord your God is giving you" (Exodus 20:12). The Fourth Commandment isn't just for the parents' benefit. It's for the benefit of all of us, the children and parents. Right relationship with our parents is essential for the quality of our own lives. It profoundly affects our life with God and with other people.

Communication is a vital part of our relationship with our parents. Some years ago, a man came to me, very distraught. His father had died a few days before. The death had been sudden, so quick that the son never had the chance to say some last words to him. The son was upset because there were things he had wanted to tell his father: an apology for certain things he'd regretted saying to his father, a request for forgiveness for some hurtful things that the son felt he'd done to his father. I told the man that he could still say these words to his father: He should take some time to sit quietly and, in a prayerful spirit, imagine that his father was sitting across from him. He should then say all those things that he had wanted to say to his father, but hadn't. And then he should allow his father to speak to him in reply. The man did this meditation and found it to be a healing experience. It lifted a great burden from his heart.

What burdens might we still be carrying from our relationship with our parents? What forgiveness do we need to ask of them? What things need to be said that we haven't said? It's usually best to say these things to our parents while they are alive. If your parents are still alive, what do you need to tell them today? Your own peace and happiness may be at stake here. Even if your parents have died, however, you can still communicate these things to them now, because they are one with us in Christ.

Our relationship with our parents is our "source" relationship. It affects every relationship we will have in life. This is especially true if there is something in our relationship with our parents that needs healing. Until our relationship with our parents is healed, we can never really have a relationship with anyone else.[1] Suppose my parents abused me when I was a child. They put me down with their words, hurt me, made me feel worthless. Until my wounds from that abuse are healed, I will never have a real relationship with another person. I will carry my resentment and hurt into every friendship, marriage, and relationship that I have for the rest of my life. And so every time I feel threatened or hurt by my spouse, those old buttons will be pushed. I'll react blindly, like the wounded child that I still am. Instead of relating to my spouse, I'll continue to react to my hurtful parent who may be long dead.

Until our relationship with our parents is healed, we will never have another relationship. Any other relationship will always be just a rehash of the wounded one we have with our parents. Even our relationship with God will be twisted and distorted by a damaged relationship with our parents.

We honor our father and our mother by forgiving them for any and every hurt we have ever received from them. Our very life can depend on this. Medical studies show that anger is a killer emotion. It can make us ill, give us cancer. Holding on to anger is like continually ingesting poison. Over time it does great harm to us.

Ask yourself, "What things do I need to forgive my parents for?" Take some time for quiet prayer and express that forgiveness to them. Give your forgiveness unconditionally, with nothing held back: no "ifs," "ands," or "buts." For those of you who have experienced a great deal of hurt, forgiveness may take some time. It may even be a while before you're ready to forgive. This can be a process. But it is a process that we must undergo. Our well-being depends on it.

Once we have allowed our relationship with our parents to be healed, we can hear an even deeper and more demanding meaning to the Fourth Commandment: We are to let go of every way in which we live life like a dependent little child. We give true honor to our parents when we grow to be the fully alive sons and daughters God wants us to be.

One way that we can live as dependent children is to be in continual reaction to things. Our whole existence can be a reaction to something, rather than a creation. Maybe somebody humiliated us in the second grade, and in our shame we withdrew from life. Ever since then we've held ourselves back, never allowing ourselves to be truly alive, because we're afraid of being shamed again.

Or, when we were young, we found that if we were always pleasing to our parents, they would never be angry with us. And so to this day we live life as the great pleaser, wanting everyone to like us. We're still that pleasing little child.

Or maybe in our childhood we concluded that life is not fair, that life can be hurtful, and in anger we began to blame something or somebody else for our misery. And so we spend the rest of our days reacting to our irritation with life. "Life's not fair, so I'm going to stand over here in the corner and complain about everything."

Life *isn't* fair. So, early in life, usually in our childhood, we decide upon a strategy, a reaction to life's pain. We choose some means that allows us to survive the difficulty. We withhold ourselves from life, or we become the pleaser so that we'll never be hurt, or we blame and complain. Our strategy allows us to survive, but we never grow into the creative son or daughter of God that we are called to be.

We have to ask ourselves: What is my survival strategy? In what way am I living my life as a reaction? To notice those things, and to begin to let go of them, is true conversion.

We want to hold something or somebody else responsible for our misery, but unless we choose to be responsible, we'll never grow up. There's a story I heard somewhere, about a construction worker. At lunchtime one day on the job, the worker opened his lunch box and said, "Oh, no, chicken salad again!" The next day he had chicken salad, and he reacted the same way. The same thing happened on the next day after that, and the next. Finally, a co-worker who heard these repeated complaints said, "If you can't stand the chicken salad, why don't you get your wife to make you something else for lunch?" The man replied, "Oh, I'm not married. I make these lunches myself."[2]

That's a funny story, but there's a tremendous amount of truth in it. We play the victim. We live as if we're buffeted and bruised by this arbitrary world. "My boss is a tyrant." "My spouse drives me nuts." "Things are terrible; nothing's gone right today." We look outside ourselves for the source of our unhappiness, but we're looking in the wrong place. The source is always within us. We grow when we realize that we are the ones who are generating our bitterness, our resentment, our irritation, our hostility, our fear. But this insight doesn't come easily. The fact is, we usually gain some perverse satisfaction by holding on to our debilitating thoughts and emotions. It feels good to be able to blame others for our unhappiness. It allows us not to have to be responsible for our life. And we don't want to let go of our fear, because we're used to living a fearful life; it's familiar. It may be the only life we've ever known. What would our life be like if we were free of our fear? Are we committed to finding the answer to that question, or do we want to remain a helpless casualty of life?

Our growth begins when we acknowledge that we're responsible for the obsessive fear that overwhelms us, the resentment that strangles us, the guilt that cripples us—all of it; that it's all coming from within us and nowhere else. Our growth deepens when we're committed to observing it all, every day, instead of allowing it to victimize us.

The Commandment to honor our father and mother calls us to an enormous maturity. It requires our willingness to take responsibility for our life, to admit that no event or circumstance, and no other person, has charge of our life. We alone are responsible.

We give true honor to our father and mother when we allow our wounded relationship with them to be healed, and when we consent to give up everything that keeps us living like a dependent little child. The Fourth Commandment goes to our very core, our source, and calls us to honestly examine what is happening there. What is at stake is nothing less than our life, the abundant life that God offers us.

10

Kindness from
the Beginning

~

W e Christians can sometimes misunderstand Jesus' death and Resurrection. We can have the mistaken notion that these grace-filled events were isolated occurrences in God's otherwise troubled dealings with the world; that the love extended to us in Jesus was an uncharacteristic gift from a God who is generally displeased with us.

The thinking goes something like this: In the beginning, God created the universe, and everything was good. God was pleased. But then human beings fouled things up. Adam and Eve sinned, and God was greatly displeased. In anger, God condemned humanity to a life of suffering and toil. Creation, the physical realm, now became the fallen world—a source of temptation and sin. This woeful situation continued for thousands of years until God graciously gave us a second chance by sending his Son, the long-awaited savior. The Son, to appease the Father's righteous wrath, sacrificed himself in death. This offering gave God his pound of flesh, and God's fury was abated. The gates of heaven were now opened to us and will remain open, provided we behave ourselves.

For the most part, this is a terribly distorted understanding of salvation history. The Jesus event wasn't an isolated case in God's relationship to the world. No, it was yet another act of kindness from a God who had been consistently kind from the very beginning.

I remember reading, some time ago, a magazine article about the evolution of the universe. The article quoted several scientists who, from their studies of the cosmos, had reached this conclusion: that from the very beginning the universe was oriented toward the creation of life, and toward the eventual evolution of life, which itself would be able to observe the universe. In other words, from the very start, creation was meant to be shared. God wanted life to evolve to such an extent that it too could see the wonder of the universe. From the start, creation was an act of love. Christ wasn't a onetime gift of an otherwise irate God. God was always reaching out to the world through Christ: "In the beginning was the Word....All things came into being through him" (John 1:1, 3).

God's love didn't stop with creation. It never stopped. God's kindness continued in the special relationship—the covenant—with Abraham, a humble nomadic peasant. It continued with the deliverance of the Israelites from slavery in Egypt, and their rescue from exile in Babylonia. The Jesus event, even though magnificent and unexpected, was yet another act of kindness by a God who had been steadfastly generous from day one.

Think about the kindest person whom you know. What makes that person worthy of being called "kind"? It's not one great generous act that makes someone a kind person; it's a whole series of kind acts, big and small. In the same way, it isn't just Jesus' death and Resurrection that make God kind and loving. It's God's loving acts from the very beginning and all throughout the history of the universe that show God to be compassionate.

What about today? Is God still the same loving God today? Or has God grown angry? The answer seems obvious: God is just as loving now as ever. But is that really our answer? Let's rephrase the question: Does God keep track of the bad things we do? Does God reward us when we do good and punish us when we do bad things? Now, perhaps, we're not so sure of our answer.

To find a solution to these questions, we should begin by recalling the standard of love that God asks us to follow. May we keep track of the wrongs that other people do to us? May we punish others for the hurts they inflict on us? What do the Scriptures say? When our brother or sister wrongs us, we are to forgive not seven times but seventy times seven times (Matthew 18:22). The love we are to have for one another must be forever patient, kind, without grudge or resentment (1 Corinthians 13:4-8). To put it another way, love means that we do not keep a ledger of the hurtful things other people do to us. Our forgiveness must know no limits. This is the sort of love we Christians are to give to others. This is the love that God asks of us.

So to return to our original question: Does God keep a ledger of our wrongs? If we answer yes, we are saying that God is not as loving as we are to be. God is not as forgiving as we are to be. We are to love one another unconditionally, but God "loves" us on the condition that we behave properly. God counts our misdeeds against us. God keeps a journal of our transgressions. God doesn't practice what God preaches. John, who said that "God is love" (1 John 4:8), had it wrong. God is more accountant than lover. And so we're right back to a distorted understanding of salvation: God is angry with us.

We might consider another question: What about hell? Don't people go to hell for mortal sins? Are there no consequences to our sins? And, further, how does judgment come into all of this? We're going to be judged, aren't we?

We have to be careful when we consider hell and Final Judgment, because it's easy to become fixated on those things. As a wise old Protestant pastor once told me, "People who are preoccupied with hell generally have somebody else in mind." Hell becomes the place for the people we hate the most.

I like C.S. Lewis's portrayal of hell in his book *The Great Divorce*. The book uses metaphor to describe heaven and hell. Those who are entering heaven are walking deeper and deeper into spectacularly beautiful mountains. The people who are in hell live in a dreary valley, never wanting to venture into the beauty of the neighboring mountains. These people in the valley can't stand one another. They are continually moving their homes farther and farther apart in order to put as much distance as possible between themselves. They're alone, isolated, relating to no one. That's hell: no authentic relationship to anyone, no celebration, no joy. The people in hell prefer their misery. They don't want to reach out to anyone.

I think that's a pretty credible depiction of hell. God doesn't sentence people to hell. We *choose* hell when we reject love. Like the father who let the prodigal son squander his share of the inheritance (Luke 15:11-32), God allows us to make choices and to face the consequences of our choices. If we want to live a self-centered or mediocre life, God lets us make that choice. God will give us all manner of messages and hints that our life is off track. But God will not force our freedom. We punish ourselves when we make bad choices. It is not

God who condemns: "God did not send the Son into the world to condemn the world, but in order that the world might be saved through him" (John 3:17). God sent the Son so we might finally get the picture of the incredible love that has always been given to us.

The only real problem here is that we don't believe this good news. In fact, it's too good to be true. And because we don't believe that such a love can exist for us or for others, we hold on to grudges, we repay hurts, we destroy relationships, we commit acts of violence and war. We separate ourselves from the God who can do nothing but love.

However, try as we might, we can never put ourselves beyond God's forgiveness. As it was from the beginning, God is forever reaching out to us, forever waiting for our return. We can expect nothing else from this God who "so loved the world."

Some people have asked me, "What about the stories in the Bible where God mows down the Philistines?" We have to be careful about how we interpret the Bible. The Bible is not a history book; it is not a newspaper account. The Bible is literature. It's divinely inspired literature, but it is still literature. It is a work of faith, written for people of faith. We get into trouble when we take the Bible literally.

The ancient Israelites lived in a very violent time when war was commonplace. Victory in war was necessary for a nation's survival. And so the Israelites, in their early understanding of God, interpreted God's fidelity to them in light of their situation: God's fidelity meant that God took their side in war. The underlying truth of these biblical stories is that God is always faithful, always with us. But in our Christian understanding, we know that God loves the Philistines as much as God loves the Israelites or anyone else.

But what about the earthquakes and the other calamities

that we've been seeing recently? Aren't they a sign of something? Some people like to conclude that these calamities are signs of God's disapproval, God's punishment of the sinful world. However, these things have been happening for millions of years. Consider that eons ago, a meteor or some other type of cataclysm wiped out the dinosaurs. Yet what could the dinosaurs have possibly done to deserve extinction? We're on pretty shaky ground when we say that these things are punishment for sin!

We must learn to accept the mystery, to accept unknowing. God's ways are not our ways, and we cannot always understand them. Nevertheless, we can know and trust in God's love and kindness, which were there from the beginning and will endure forever.

11

Know Yourself

~

We don't have to look very far to see that obedience is on the wane in today's troubled world. The crime and drug traffic in our cities, the cutthroat competition in our society, the savage wars of recent years, and the widespread perception that there's been a general decline in moral values all serve to give evidence of this.

When I listen to young people these days, I'm often struck by how reluctant many of them are to accept Christian teaching just because parents or some other authority tells them to. They are searching for their own answers. Many people today, youth and adults alike, are simply not willing to adopt ideals and standards that someone else tries to impose on them. The threat "You had better believe and behave or you'll have the wrath of God to face" just doesn't carry much weight any longer.

Is this a completely awful development? Is the world coming to an end? No, says the prophet Jeremiah (Jeremiah 31:31-34), it's an opportunity for something entirely new: a deeper relationship, not based on our obedience but on discovering God's law as the core of who we are.

Through Jeremiah, the Lord foretold a whole new way of relating for God and the people of Israel. For centuries, God had spoken to the Israelites, hoping that they would hear. God had given them a covenant to live, laws to follow, prophetic oracles to heed. But the Israelites had not listened, they had not obeyed.

In the future, said the Lord through Jeremiah, things would be different. A new covenant would be established. Yahweh would bypass the speaking-and-listening process and put the divine will directly into Israel's heart.[1] There would be no more need for obedience, because people wouldn't be faced with having to follow an external will. God's will would be in their heart. It would be their deepest desire.

In fact, this new relationship became available to us through Christ. It is the "new and everlasting covenant" that Jesus gave us at the Last Supper.

Saint Augustine put it pretty well when he said, *Noverim me, noverim Te*"[2]—"May I know myself, may I know Thee." In knowing ourselves, we discover God and God's law. Great mystics down through the ages have echoed Augustine: Self-knowledge is the key to the spiritual life. We may finally be ready to hear this truth. The crucial task for people today is not obedience to rules and commandments but self-knowledge.

Let's consider a practical example. Suppose I have a tendency to yell at my spouse or at the other members of my family. I feel bad about this and conclude that I'm a lousy human being. And so I resolve to curb my tongue. I make up my mind not to yell at people anymore. At best, this is only a short-term solution. The vexation and rage that gave rise to my shouting sprees are still simmering within me. My willpower may prevail for a while, but that pressure cooker inside will gradually build until it explodes again.

Obedience puts a merely temporary lid on our behavior. It doesn't liberate. Only if I face my anger, watch it, experience it in all the ways it arises within me, instead of denying it, can I hope to be free of it.

Our self-knowing has global implications. The violence within each one of us is the source of the violence in our world. Saint Teresa of Avila said:

> Can any evil be greater than the evil we find
> in our own house?...Believe me, unless we
> have peace, and seek peace in our own home,
> we shall not find it in the homes of others.[3]

If we are to bring peace to our neighborhoods, our cities, our world, we have to have peace within ourselves.

Without doubt, we're experiencing a tremendous moral crisis today. Traditional moral standards seem to have been tossed out the window. Some argue that the answer to today's chaos is to return to the "family values" of forty or fifty years ago. However, things were not as idyllic fifty years ago as we might want to think. The world of yesteryear was beset with racism and brutality, just as it is today. For Christians, "family" includes not just our immediate family but the world family. And so "family values" for Christians must involve the entire Body of Christ. We cannot begin to be a world family until we have peace within.

In this century alone, approximately 110 million people have died as a result of war. This is four times as many war deaths as occurred in the previous four centuries combined, and far outstrips the proportionate rise in population over the same period.[4] Most of those deaths occurred before 1960.

What good will it do for people to return to the old, so-called "family values" when they haven't dealt with the violence within? What good will it do for people to control their household behavior while they make or sell armaments that kill people all over the globe?

It does little good to indoctrinate our children with Christian teaching when the world we've created requires that they live by a different norm. In school, our young people quickly learn that their status is determined by their popularity, their grade-point average, or their athletic achievements. This is the world we adults have set up: Who you are is measured by your importance, your wealth, your success. These are the criteria by which students begin to judge one another as potential adversaries. "To get ahead, I have to outdo the other students." The other kids in school become obstacles to a student's success.

The same holds true in so much of the workaday world. People scramble to climb the ladder of success, because their self-worth depends on it. Rules can be broken, other people can be trampled upon. We may think that this is terrible behavior, but what else can we expect once we've decided to measure people by their importance and affluence?

When there are nations filled with people struggling to get ahead of one another, it's no wonder that our world suffers from the violence of brutal competition. Nations vie for a bigger and bigger share of the economic pie. War becomes a "super bowl" that we watch on TV, a big football game in which we try to annihilate the other side to prove that we're Number 1. Again, it's a lesson we learned when we were children: Other people are obstacles to our success.

When the Christian Church tells people today to "follow God's law, love your neighbor," who is going to listen? People see that Christians are not serious about this—not when so many of them have unquestioningly accepted success and status-seeking as a way of life. Others see through such pretense.

The quest of the Christian life is to be who we already are—a wondrous creation, a son or daughter of God. It is not our job to improve or reshape ourselves. We do not have to remake ourselves so as to conform to some external standard. Instead, we are to be who we really are. When we can let go of our need to be different from who we are, we will drop the greed, the fear, and the violence that are ravaging our world. We will discover what it truly means to love our neighbor as ourself.

It's essential that we be conscious of all the ways we do attempt to recreate ourselves. Perhaps this exercise will help: Sit down and list all the ways you are trying to become more or better: in appearance, image, status, successfulness, respectability, importance; becoming a nice person, good person, holy person, and so on. Include here any need you may have to be liked or approved of by others. Do not include those things that you are trying to *do* better, such as paying attention to the present moment or job performance. But if you do measure who you are by how well you perform, then include that in this list. When your list is complete, begin to tally the cost of all your attempts to change who you are: the tremendous energy expended, the worry, the anxiety, the depression, the sleepless nights, the hurt, the isolation, the fear, the physical effects, the unhappiness. Now ask yourself: "What would my life be like if I were completely to drop my need to remake who I am?"

Obedience may work as a temporary restraint, but it will not solve the crisis in the world today. Only self-knowing will. Peace within ourselves begins with the realization that we don't have to improve who we are. We don't have to try to measure up to an external demand. Instead, we need to know ourselves.

The moral chaos in our world today is a challenge to look within. We are to face the greed, the fear, the heartless striving within us. We are to see the delusion and the violence that come from thinking that we can remake who we are. We are to see all of that, to become conscious of it nonjudgmentally. This seeing without judgment will give us true understanding of ourselves. We are liberated when we understand the roots of our striving and fear. This is by far a more demanding task than putting handcuffs on our behavior, but it is the only thing that will bring us true peace.

God's will is not an external ideal. It is our heart's desire. It's the deepest part of who we are: the "new and everlasting covenant," as foretold by Jeremiah.

12

Death and New Life

~

The universe was once viewed by scientists as a dependable, clockwork system. But new discoveries in science have demonstrated that this isn't true. The universe is filled with disorder. For example, the weather will never be as predictable as we would like. Very small changes on the earth can have an expanding impact that will produce major changes in the weather. The flap of a butterfly's wings can change the weather a month later. This is known in science as "the butterfly effect."

Traditional science once studied the human heart as if it were a pump beating like precision machinery. But hearts are far more complicated than that. Our heartbeat is triggered by signals from our brain, but the actual rhythmic contractions occur because of the consent of millions of muscle fibers, all agreeing to contract at the same time. Our heartbeat rhythm always varies by tiny amounts, even when our body is at rest.

In the midst of the universe's disorder, however, there are amazing patterns. Even though our heartbeat originates from a mob of cells, our heart can usually be relied on to give life and nourishment to our bodies. The organized form of living beings, such as dogs and cats and humans, somehow arises from the chaotic motion of cells and chemicals within those beings.

There is widespread chaos in the universe, but from that chaos emerge marvelous and even simple patterns. This is the paradox that science is now discovering and trying to understand.[1]

Chaos has been found not only in nature but also in economics and in the social relations of human beings. It's a fact of life in the universe in which we live. And it was a major factor in what took place at the first Easter.

The disciples had been left with a chaotic situation after Jesus was killed. They were greatly confused and uncertain about what had happened. They had expected Jesus to establish the Kingdom, but he died an untimely death. He was the Son of God, yet he was unjustly and horribly killed. They were traumatized by what had happened. For days afterward, they hid themselves in fear (John 20:19).

Easter morning brought wondrous order to their confusion. Yes, their Messiah had been wrongly put to death, but this dreadful crime was not the end. This awful tragedy was not the last word. God brought something marvelously good out of it all. In the Resurrection, God had the final say. Amid chaos and senseless violence, God's grace was also at work. Christ survived it all as One who loves. He was now at the heart of the universe, not a mere memory or a belief. Christ could be directly experienced as One who loves.

In our own lives, we inevitably face confusion, disarray, and even disasters. Our life can sometimes seem to be in shambles. How do we react to those things? Are we paralyzed with fear? Do we become depressed, angry, cynical, or resigned? "Oh, things are so terrible!" we think. "Everything's gone wrong." "I really got a raw deal." "I'm very upset." Sometimes it seems as if we *want* to think that that is the end of the story, that evil wins and that things won't work out.

A Chinese story tells about a farmer who had an old horse that he used to plow his fields. One day the horse ran away into the hills. The farmer's neighbors expressed pity over the farmer's bad luck, but the farmer thought, "Is this good luck or bad luck?" A few days later the horse returned, bringing with it a herd of wild horses from the hills. The neighbors now congratulated the farmer on his good fortune. But he thought, "Is this good luck or bad luck?" Later, while the farmer's son was trying to tame one of the wild horses, he fell off its back and broke his leg. Everybody thought this was a terrible thing. But again the farmer wondered, "Is this good luck or bad luck?" Several weeks later the army marched into town and drafted every able-bodied young man who could be found. When the soldiers came to the farmer's son, they saw his broken leg and let him off. Now, was that good luck or bad luck?

Jesus' Resurrection makes known to us that we need not become paralyzed by or despair over what we see as bad things happening. They are never the end. Many of us have experienced catastrophe in our lives: cancer or heart attack, death of a loved one, a child in serious trouble. I don't belittle any of these things, or the pain that can come from them. But the Resurrection tells us that there is something more, much more. God will have the final say. No matter what awful thing has happened or will happen, good can come from it. God *will* bring good out of it, if we have faith.

Some years ago, a mother told me how her young son had been crippled with the disease multiple sclerosis, and what a difficult thing this was for her son and the family to endure. But after many months, and after the family had got over the initial blow and had become better able to deal with the situation, the mother told me, "You know, before my son's illness, our family wasn't very close. We were financially well off, but there wasn't much warmth to our family life. My son's illness has forced all of us to join together. We now have a love for our son and a love for one another that we never had before."

We live in a world where there is grief, tragedy, even disaster and evil. Our Christian faith tells us that this is not simply a chaotic mess. There is a pattern to it all. The pattern is dying and rising. It is the basic design of the entire universe: death and new life. Out of the worst tragedy can come an even greater good.

Do we see this pattern at work in our lives? Each of our lives is like a beautiful vase. At a certain point, we make a major mistake in our life, or we suffer an enormous hurt or loss, and our vase becomes cracked. Over time, we may even develop many breaks and cracks. Christ's Resurrection shows us that it is in our breaks, our cracks, that Resurrection light can shine through. Our flaws become places where the beauty of our vase can be brilliantly enhanced. The more breaks there are, the more the light can shine. Where sin abounds, grace abounds all the more. Wherever our life is fractured with pain and uncertainty, it is precisely there that God's brilliance can break through.

How have we looked at the troubles and losses of our life? How have we dealt with the cracks in our vase? Have we turned them into a source of darkness? Have they become simply an excuse to be unhappy, to blame and complain, a justification for all kinds of negativity?

No greater injury was suffered by anyone in human history than that suffered by Jesus of Nazareth. No wrong ever committed was more horrendous than the crucifixion of the Son of God. Yet this awful indignity became the source of Resurrection. A terrible evil was transformed into powerful new life for all of us. This is the grand design of the universe.

The grace of new life gives us much to celebrate. It's a grace that is there for the asking, for every one of us. It's a grace that can turn any sadness into joy, and can transform darkness into marvelous light.

13

A Firsthand Faith

~

There's a story that Anthony de Mello tells about Nasruddin, a character in Indian folklore. A relative once came to visit Nasruddin, bringing a duck as a gift. Nasruddin cooked the bird and shared it with his relative. Soon one guest after another began to call, each claiming to be a friend of the friend of the "man who brought you the duck." Each one, of course, expected to be fed and housed on the strength of that duck. At length Nasruddin could stand it no longer. One day a stranger arrived at his house and said, "I am a friend of the friend of the man who brought you the duck." And, like the others, he sat down, expecting to be fed.

Nasruddin brought out a bowl of steaming hot water and placed it before him. "What is this?" asked the stranger. "This," said Nasruddin, "is the soup of the soup of the duck that was brought to me by my relative."[1]

As Christians, we can be tempted to settle for a watered-down, secondhand faith. We may hold our Christian faith only because the apostles said it was true, or because our parents or our teachers or someone else said it was true. But if we don't make our faith our own, it's just secondhand. We can never be convinced of our faith until it's based on our direct experience and not just on what someone else has said. We are all, to an extent, like the apostle Thomas, who required physical evidence of the Lord's Resurrection because he was unable to accept it on faith alone.

In John 20:19-31, the other disciples kept telling Thomas, "We've seen the Lord; He is Risen!" Thomas, however, refused to yield to this constant pressure to believe. He insisted that he see the Risen Jesus for himself.

He's called "Doubting Thomas," which usually carries a derogatory connotation. We tend to look down on Thomas's attitude because he so stubbornly resisted the truth of Christ's Resurrection until he was given palpable proof.

Thomas should be admired, however. He refused to believe something just because other people said it was true. He demanded that he be given a personal, firsthand experience of the Risen Jesus before he would believe.

He got what he demanded. The Risen Christ appeared to him and said, "Take your finger and examine my hands. Put your hand into my side." And because of this profound, direct encounter with the Risen Christ, Thomas not only believed, he was *convinced* about the Resurrection. He made what is probably the strongest profession of faith recorded in the gospels: "My Lord and my God." He was so convinced of Christ's Resurrection that, unlike the rest of the apostles, who stayed closer to home, he traveled all the way to India (as tradition tells us) to preach the Good News. All of this happened because Thomas was insistent enough to demand a personal faith experience. He was bold enough to take Jesus up on his offer, "Ask and you shall receive."

Thomas is an example to all of us. He challenges us never

A FIRSTHAND FAITH ~ 85

to found our faith simply on what other people have told us
to be true. We have to make our faith our own. I have to
make "my own" what I say I believe as a Christian.

This can be difficult. We can be confronted with the same
thing Thomas had to face when he encountered the other
apostles: "You should believe what the group believes; you
should believe because those who are in the know tell you it's
true." But if we satisfy ourselves with believing something
only because other people have told us it's true, then our faith
is secondhand.

Here is the account of a young woman who is a wife and
mother. She relates her journey from a secondhand faith to a
faith based on direct experience:

> Until I was thirty, God played hardly any part
> in my life. I come from an "average Christian
> family" in which we went to church on Sun-
> days if nothing else seemed more important
> at the time, but my parents readily missed
> Mass in order to go swimming or skiing.
> When I was a child and wanted to go to Mass
> anyway, I had to fight many a battle and had
> many arguments with my parents. But I was
> really going to Mass only from fear of hell. In
> my youth and as an adult I kept up the prac-
> tice of Mass, occasional Communion and
> confession, and a short period of daily prayer.
> Nonetheless God was not important to me.

While she was in her thirties, this woman began an intense practice of contemplative prayer that changed her life.
In her journal, she describes her experience while on a contemplative retreat:

> The morning meditation was very beautiful. Again I felt one with the "Thou"—although now and then a few disturbing thoughts showed up.
>
> I would really prefer not to write at all, since nothing I write down can ever express what I have received. The "Thou" is God; he is in me and I can be in him, always and everywhere, wherever I go and whatever I do. At every moment I rejoice in my being, which has its ground in him. I will go back once again to ordinary life; nothing seems to have changed, and yet everything has changed.

After the retreat had ended and she had returned to her family, she wrote:

> I am gradually getting used to home again; I do my work, I cook and clean, I talk to the children and my husband, I go shopping. But in reality I have passed almost completely into the possession of God. He alone occupies me, challenges me, repeatedly shows me that I belong to him not only during meditation but throughout the day. I feel his presence....
>
> There is no difference between meditation and everyday life—everything is "Thou."[2]

We tend to think that such experiences are exceptional, reserved only for those few who have special spiritual gifts. To a certain extent at least, this is a misconception. The Second Vatican Council made it clear that there are no preordained grades of holiness for people. There is a universal call to holiness for all Christians.[3] Although each of our experiences will be different, every one of us, by reason of our baptism, is called to a genuine experience of God. God wants every one of us to know firsthand the divine Presence in our lives. As the Trappist monk Thomas Keating says, "The presence of God should become a kind of fourth dimension" to our entire life.[4]

A few years ago some atheists staged a political rally somewhere in the South. The rally was led by Madeleine Murray O'Hare, national spokesperson for atheists. She carried a sign that read, "I don't believe in God because I don't believe in the Easter bunny." When we hear of something like that, are we threatened or disturbed? If we are threatened, do we try to push that message out of our mind? Or do we honestly try to deal with the doubts that arise from that disturbing message? Do we learn from Thomas's example by trying to resolve those doubts, especially through prayer? Do we seek our own answers about whether God exists?

If someone says to us, "The sun doesn't exist; the sun doesn't come up in the morning," we're not troubled by that. We know the sun exists; we experience it every day. We don't get so upset when someone questions something that we know from our everyday life. However, we do become disturbed about things that we hope are true but that we don't know firsthand. When someone questions our secondhand beliefs, we feel threatened. Let's ask ourselves, "Do I react emotionally when my Christian faith is attacked or contradicted or questioned?" If the answer is "yes," that's a pretty good indication that what we believe is largely secondhand. But we don't need to despair, because Thomas points the way for us. Our doubts are an occasion for us to question, to investigate, to pray. It's especially important that we practice some form of listening prayer, such as Centering Prayer or Breathing Prayer (see Appendix II). That's true faith in action.

A real problem arises when we rely on the Church for all the answers. The laity have the questions, and the clergy have the answers, or so the thinking goes. The laity can rest easy, because the clergy supposedly have answers even for those questions that haven't yet been asked or thought of! "All is well and secure, because the Church has all the solutions." Too much of what passes for Christian faith can be based simply on what someone else has said. It's a faith founded on someone else's convictions, rather than the answers we have made our own.

There is another movement today, however. Karl Rahner, S.J., has predicted, "The Christian of the future will be a mystic, or he or she will not exist at all."[5] By "mystic" Rahner meant a person with a genuine experience of God in ordinary life. A growing number of people today are searching for such experience. They refuse to be satisfied with what someone else tells them to be true. They will not believe something they cannot experience.

Some people lament this development. They long for the "good old days" when one believed what one was taught, no questions asked. But if Karl Rahner is right, as I think he is, we can never go back to those days. We can never go back! The days of a secondhand faith are fading into memory. And rightly so, because every one of us has been sealed with the Spirit. Every one of us has the responsibility to seek answers to our doubts and questions, to make our Christian faith our own. Each of us is called to bring a contemplative dimension into the heart of our daily life. We are to be those blessed ones who have not seen the Risen Christ, yet believe because of a profound sense of Christ's presence in our life.

Saint Thomas shows us that questioning is necessary if our

faith is to be sound. Our qualms and uncertainties call us to a deeper experience of the Risen Christ. Thomas challenges us never to be satisfied with a watered-down faith, never to base our faith simply upon what other people have said. Like Saint Thomas, we must be demanding, we must always seek to make our faith our own, so that, with him, we may say from the depths of our hearts, "My Lord and my God!"

14

The Silence
of Unknowing

~

Ignorance is a state of being unaware of something. What causes ignorance? The problem isn't just a lack of information. Ignorance isn't caused by what we don't know. Ignorance results from what we think we know. Our judgments, conclusions, and opinions about things block our receptiveness to anything new.

We often see this played out in relationships. To a great extent, we can relate to one another on the basis of an image. If I see Frank acting in a foolish way, I form an image about him from that incident. From that time on, whenever I see Frank, that image comes to mind: "Frank is an idiot." I don't relate to Frank, I relate to my idea about him.

Spouses can struggle with such stereotypes. It's easy to get into the rut of thinking, "I've been married to him (her) for twenty years; I know him (her). I've got him (her) figured out. Nothing surprising is going to come from him (her)." As soon as spouses think like that, their relationship begins to wither. The same holds true for any relationship.

We label and package people on the basis of our conclusions about them. We relate to them out of our prior judgments or pre-set images, or on the basis of their past behavior. That's ignorance. The other person may have changed since we saw him or her last, but we won't hear of it, we won't allow it, because we know what that person is really like. Or so we think.

There's a story about a man named Harry who suffered from a terribly closed mind. One night Harry was awakened by a visit from the Lord, who called, "Harry, Harry."

"Who is it?" Harry demanded.

"I am the One Who Is," said the Lord.

"Oh, no," said Harry with disgust, "I don't believe it."

The Lord said, "I've come to talk to you, Harry, about a man who never listens to anything or anybody, a man who lives in his own world."

"I don't believe it," Harry repeated as he pulled the pillow over his ears to block out what he was hearing. The next morning at the office, Harry complained to a co-worker, "I swear, somehow my ex-wife got into the house last night. I couldn't believe it. And she's still harping on the same old thing. She hasn't changed a bit!"

What we know is ultimately a barrier to drawing close to God. Some of the people who caused Jesus to be killed were pious souls, steeped in religious knowledge. They *knew* that God would never associate with prostitutes, tax collectors, and reprobates. They *knew* that nobody important could ever come from Nazareth. They *knew* that someone as familiar as the son of Joseph the carpenter couldn't have anything significant to say. They killed the Author of Life because they were blinded by their "knowledge."

Other people of that time were convinced that the Messiah would be a strong political figure who would help Israel throw off Roman rule. They *knew* that the real Messiah would never counsel them to "love your enemies."

In the Emmaus story (Luke 24:13-35), the disciples at first failed to recognize Jesus because they were sure he was dead. It was unthinkable that he could now be walking alongside of them on the road. Jesus' Incarnation had shown the world that God's presence could be found in human form; that human flesh, and indeed the whole universe, is shot through with divine light. Yet the disciples failed to see this. Their vision was clouded by their own preconceptions.

Christ is to be found in other people; God can be discovered in the wonder of creation. Yet we are ignorant of this presence because of what we think we know.

A number of years ago, I was an associate pastor in a large parish. One Holy Saturday afternoon, some members of the parish were in the church, preparing things for the Easter services that would take place that weekend. They were putting up banners, getting the baptismal font ready, and placing new candles in the church. They had placed about three dozen Easter lilies in the sanctuary. The flowers were magnificent. I remember a boy, perhaps ten years old, who seemed to be transfixed by their beauty. He stood looking at the flowers for the longest while. Meanwhile, the adults were all busy with their work. Finally, the boy looked up and asked, "What kind of flowers are these?" One of the adults shrugged and said, "Oh, they're Easter lilies. You've seen Easter lilies before, haven't you?" Everyone else knew what kind of flowers they were, but apparently only the boy saw their beauty.

The Indian mystic Krishnamurti said, "Once you teach a child that the bird is a 'sparrow,' the child never again sees the bird." We live in an artificial world of labels and words. That's ignorance. We name, classify, categorize, and pigeonhole everything, and then dismiss it with the thought, "I know it now, so there's nothing more to see." Ignorance is the state of being stuck in what we know, instead of living with what's real.

Faith is not just belief. It's not just holding certain doctrines and creeds. Faith is also an openness to living without knowing, a commitment to being with what cannot be known. It means quieting our thinking so that we can be with other people as they are, instead of remaining fixed on our image of them. It means experiencing life as it is, instead of being caught up in our endless judgments and opinions about it.

Ultimately, what we know is a hindrance to knowing God. Saint John of the Cross said that to attain union with God, we "must advance by unknowing, rather than by knowing."[1] In the Emmaus story, we are told that the disciples' eyes were finally opened, and they recognized Jesus, but that as soon as they did so, "he vanished from their sight" (Luke 24:31). As soon as we think we have the truth, it slips out of our grasp. The moment we think we've got God or other people or the world figured out, we've lost sight of the gospel. An enormous amount of violence and war and bigotry has been committed in human history by people who thought they were doing God's will. It continues to happen today.

Faith requires that we let go of the presumption that we know. What is hidden from the learned and the clever *is* revealed to the merest children.

Faith is an invitation always to suspend our conclusions and opinions, so that we may behold the marvel of each moment. That's the good news of the Resurrection: that each moment, each created thing, is now a source of wonder for us. Within each moment there is something inexpressible. We can come upon this wonder when we live in the silence of unknowing. As Saint John Chrysostom once said:

Hades is angered because it has been frustrated, it is angered because it has been mocked, it is angered because it has been destroyed; it is angered because it has been reduced to naught, it is angered because it is now captive. It seized a body, and lo! it discovered God; it seized earth, and behold! it encountered heaven; it seized the visible, and was overcome by the invisible. O death, where is your sting? O Hades, where is your victory?[2]

15

The True Shepherd

~

We have one Shepherd who leads us, who alone can guide us to fullness of life. There is one Shepherd, and there is no other (John 10:11-14). Isn't it the case, though, that we spend a lot of energy seeking answers from other voices, searching for relief somewhere else?

Today, it seems that wherever there are reports of apparitions of some saint, people flock to the site seeking a miracle. We are captivated by the mysterious and the miraculous. We want a cure for the emptiness of our lives, and we think we can get it from some otherworldly source. But the true Shepherd is not to be found in a fascinating miracle in some distant place. The true Shepherd is right here, right now, in each moment of our lives. Often, that's the last place we want to look.

Much of what passes for religious faith today is actually just a desire for something elaborate or attractive or puzzling. The mystic Ramana Maharshi put it this way:

> For example, many Christians won't be satis-
> fied unless they are told that God is some-
> where in the far-off heavens, not to be reached
> by us unaided... If they are told the simple
> truth that "the Kingdom of Heaven is within
> you" [see Luke 17:21] they will not be satis-
> fied, and will read complex and far-fetched
> meanings into it. Only mature minds can
> grasp the truth in all its simplicity.[1]

In my own life, I sometimes catch myself thinking, "I wish I could find some saintly, enlightened master to study with"— preferably someone in a far-distant country, with a heavy Asian accent, someone who could show me all the techniques for spiritual advancement, someone who would give me all the answers I need. In other words, I want a different Shepherd from the one who is right here, right now.

Some years ago, Mother Teresa gave a talk in a large city. There was a multimillionaire in her audience who was truly impressed by her words and her presence. After she had fin-ished speaking, the wealthy man came up to Mother Teresa and asked if he could accompany her to her next destination. He wanted to be around this saintly woman for a while longer. But Mother Teresa refused his request, saying, "Stay here and use what you have to help people here."

We already have within us the resources and gifts of the Kingdom. We sometimes think that someone else can give us the peace and joy we want, but it's all right here.

Even if we're not seeking a saint or guru to give us solu-tions to our life, we may be clinging to some other person for security and fulfillment. We want to find that one true love who will make us happy. We seek out friends who will like us, affirm us, insulate us from the pain of life. We avoid people who don't fill these needs for us. Our relationships become a means to escape life.

Recently, I was speaking with a married couple whom I know. They have had six children. Five of their children are now grown up and on their own. Their youngest child is still in high school and lives at home. The parents told me, "We're trying to raise our daughter so that she will no longer need us." What a healthy approach! They don't want their daughter to remain psychologically dependent on them. They want their daughter to be free of them. Only when we are free of the need to cling to other people can we begin to love other people. This is gospel love: love without clinging dependence, love without making other people objects to fill our needs.

How can we learn to love that way? We don't have to search outside ourselves. This treasure-house is within us. The Shepherd is with us in each moment. Each moment is our teacher if we are willing to watch and listen. We'd rather not look into our everyday thoughts, feelings, and actions, but that is precisely where the true voice is to be found. Our animosity, our envy, our arrogance—each of these is an occasion to notice and listen. Each is an opportunity to learn wisdom from the Shepherd. The Shepherd is to be found in our watching and listening.

The root meaning of the word "observe" comes from a Latin word (*servare*) that means "to shepherd, to watch, to guard." When we really observe our daily lives, with all the stuff we find there, no matter how distasteful or disheartening that might seem, we're being attentive to the Shepherd. If we have the discipline to watch and watch and watch, we'll see where we need to alter our course, where we are to find the right paths. We'll discover the peace that is already within us. In the secrets of our heart, God will teach us wisdom (Psalm 51:6). The wisdom of the Shepherd is to be found in everyday watchfulness. Attentiveness brings about change in our lives, slowly but powerfully.

There's a beautiful story about a man who owned a family business. One year he went away on a long trip, and he left one of his sons in charge of the business. After the father had been gone for some time, the son began to steal money from the business. Months later, the father returned and learned about the son's thievery. But he said nothing to his son. The young man continued to steal, while the father only watched. Finally, the son realized that his father knew all about his embezzling. The son grew ashamed of what he had been doing. And so he began to pay back the money. He paid and paid until he made up for everything he had stolen. In time he became the most dedicated and conscientious worker in his father's business.

Self-observation brings about true change in us. We notice all those things about ourselves that are robbing us of life. If we observe ourselves long enough and fully enough, we're likely to cry an ocean of tears over what we see: the hurts we've held on to, the harm we've inflicted on others, the sadness we've stored up over the years. The mystics call this the "gift of tears." This is transformation.

It can be demanding discipline to remain attentive to the Shepherd. And because it's hard, we yearn for those far-off, mysterious, miraculous voices that we think will give us relief. All the while, we're looking in the wrong place. We need look nowhere else than the everyday circumstances and relationships of our life. It's here that we can find this Kingdom that is with us, within us. It's here that we can listen to the Shepherd who knows us more intimately than we know ourselves.

16

The Illusion
of Separateness

~

I n the state of Washington, there is a spectacular rain
forest on the Olympic Peninsula. Climate, terrain, and
geographical location have combined to make it one
of the few temperate rain forests in the world. Approximately
twelve feet of rain fall there every year. Everywhere you look
in that forest, there is life. Countless species of wildlife and
vegetation flourish there; even the surfaces of the rocks and
trees are crammed with moss or tiny insects.

There's a real fragility to the things that live in that rain
forest. They are all in a delicate balance of interrelationship.
For example, if the trees adjacent to a stream are destroyed,
the water temperature will rise because of the reduced shade,
which in turn will kill the fish, which will in turn affect the
survival of the otter and the bear and the eagle that eat the
fish. If the yearly rainfall in the forest drops significantly, less
moss will carpet the trees, providing less winter food for the
many animals that eat the moss. The survival of one species

affects the entire forest, just as a change in climate or vegetation affects every living thing in the forest.

We are like the living things in that forest: We flourish when we live out of a profound sense of interconnectedness with one another. We don't have life outside of that relationship to one another. Without one another, we have no hope of becoming the people we were created to be. We do harm to ourselves when we try to live under the illusion that we are separate individuals.

In his last discourse (John 15:5), Jesus spoke to his gathered disciples, not as individuals, but as a group, a community: "Together, you are the branches. I am the vine," Jesus told them. Only when we recognize this deep interconnection do we truly have life. When we hold on to the idea that we are separate from one another, we wither.

Separateness *is* an illusion, and one that is being confirmed by science. For years, scientists tried to discover the smallest particle of matter, the ultimate building block of the universe. The atom was first thought to be that building block. Then subatomic particles were discovered. Later on, quarks were found. And now, some quantum physicists conclude that there is *no* independent, ultimate particle of matter. If you can look at what seems to be the smallest particle of matter, what you discover is not one isolated particle, but a host of particles that interact and depend upon one another for their very existence. In other words, the ultimate building block of matter is relationship.[1] What we see in rain forests and human relations is a reflection of what is happening in the most minute particles of our world. There is nothing separate or independent in reality. All is relationship.

We go through life with the idea that "I" am a separate entity, that there is this independent "me" that I have to be concerned about: my private life, my needs, my wants, my

career, my advancement. In fact, there is no "me" that is separate from the rest of creation. Everything is relationship.
Whatever is not in relationship does not exist. To exist is to
be in relationship. We are in constant affiliation with other
people, and with the earth and other physical things. We need
air to breathe, food to eat, water to drink, the sun to provide
us with light and warmth. We are intimately connected with
the rest of the cosmos. When we forget this, our very survival
is put in jeopardy, as is happening today with the environ-
mental crisis.

And so, without relationship none of us has life. When we
actually realize this, our relationships with our spouse, our
family, our friends, our parish, and with the rest of the human
race become critically important. Relationships are an ongoing
challenge to live in reality, to drop the illusion of separateness.

Relationships offer us a growing awareness of what's real.
This can be painful work. A man who had been a habitual
drinker once told me, "When I was still drinking, I was a
drunken, obnoxious SOB. Now that I've given up drinking,
my wife tells me that I'm just an obnoxious SOB." It would
have been easy for him to think, "Now that I've quit drinking, I've solved all my problems." But his wife kept him honest. Relationships will do that for us. It's like looking in the
mirror. Before we go out of the house in the morning, we look
in the mirror to comb our hair and make sure that our clothes
look nice. The mirror gives us an accurate reflection of our
physical appearance. In the same way, relationships can give
us a mirror image of what we are really like at every moment:
our self-preoccupation, our attachments, our irritableness. For
our part, we have to be willing to look in the mirror.

Our relatedness brings us into reality, provided we are open
to it. For instance, we prefer to avoid those people who an-
noy us, upset us, rub us the wrong way, push our buttons. Yet

these are precisely the people who can help us to grow. Our reaction to them exposes the egoism we try to hide, the fear we suppress, the spite we pretend isn't there. Let's ask ourselves, "Who is the person I most hate to be around?" We need that very person in order to be real. As long as we feel we can't be around that person, there will be a part of us that is withering on the vine.

Relationships show us what's truly happening in our life, if we have the courage to face it. They reveal this separate, unreal self of ours who wants to isolate us from the rest of the human race. If you've been married or have maintained a friendship with someone through thick and thin, you know this to be true. Our relationships continually expose this little "me" who wants things "my" own way, who seeks to dominate, manipulate, possess, control. Relationships are a daily call to die to our separate self.

If we come to church on Sunday with the notion, "I'm here to be alone with God, I'm here to do my private devotion," we're living in a dream world. There is no such thing as a solitary Christian. The Catholic Church says that the Eucharist is the "summit and source" of our life and worship. This is because the Eucharist points us to ultimate truth: our oneness in Christ. Everything contrary to that is an illusion. Whatever aversion we have to being a member of a faith community, whatever dislike we have about taking part in the Eucharist as a community celebration—all of that is an opportunity to become aware, to live in reality, to drop the illusion of separateness.

Christ is the vine, we are the branches. The branches are in fact the whole human race. The fact is that we are in profound kinship to the entire planet. The Trappist monk Thomas Merton once had a momentous experience of this. In his earlier years, he had joined the monastery as a way of seeking

holiness, believing that union with God required that he withdraw himself from the everyday world. But one day while he
was walking on a crowded street in Louisville, Kentucky, something happened that altered his perspective radically. He
tells of this event in his book *Conjectures of a Guilty Bystander*:

> In Louisville, at the corner of Fourth and Wal-
> nut, in the center of the shopping district, I
> was suddenly overwhelmed with the realiza-
> tion that I loved all those people, that they
> were mine and I theirs, that we could not be
> alien to one another even though we were
> total strangers. It was like waking from a
> dream of separateness, of spurious self-isola-
> tion in a special world, the world of renun-
> ciation and supposed holiness. The whole il-
> lusion of a separate holy existence is a
> dream...There is no way of telling people that
> they are all walking around shining like the
> sun....There are no strangers!...If only we
> could see each other [as we really are] all the
> time. There would be no more war, no more
> hatred, no more cruelty, no more greed....I
> suppose the big problem would be that we
> would fall down and worship each
> other....The gate of heaven is everywhere.[2]

This overwhelming realization changed Merton's life forever. He never again looked on his monastic vocation as a
withdrawal from the world. He became deeply concerned
about issues of peace, justice, and racism. What other choice
did he have, now that he saw himself in every victim of war,

in every starving child, in every person of another race? He had no other choice.

Christ is the vine, we are the branches. We labor under the delusion that we are isolated from other people. The consequences are fear, suspicion, and conflict—all of which are destroying our world today. Imagine what would happen if people were to drop this fantasy of separateness. What if even just the Christians were to let go of this delusion? What if we were to move beyond our little, separate self to discover our true Self, this shining sun that each of us is? There would be a revolution, in the best sense of that word, in our world. Think of it. Our world would be changed forever.

The gospel image of the vine and the branches is a wake-up call for all of us. It is an invitation to live the reality of our deep connection with all of creation. It is a reminder to allow our everyday relationships with spouse, friend, co-worker, and community to point the way to an awareness of our ultimate interrelatedness. It is a plea to drop our illusions, and live the truth of our oneness in Christ.

17

One in the Spirit

~

Peter and the other believers had a startling revelation: Gentiles had received the Holy Spirit (Acts10:44-48). The grace of the Risen Christ was not meant just for the children of Abraham. Jews, and Jewish Christians, who were the chosen people by reason of an age-old covenant, no longer had an exclusive claim on God's favor.

This event brought home to Peter and the early Christians the surprising truth about the God who had raised Jesus from the dead: that God makes no distinction among persons. All are part of the Kingdom. The Spirit can be given to anybody and everybody.

Some years ago, I gave a talk about the Catholic Church. I pointed out that it now sees that the Protestant churches are part of God's Kingdom too, which evoked this comment from a listener: "I can accept the notion that the Protestants are saved too, but it's still not easy to do so. There was always a certain satisfaction in believing that we Catholics were the only saved ones, and the rest of the human race was going to hell."

It seems to be an eternal temptation for Christians to think that we're the saved ones, and everyone else is excluded. We like to set ourselves apart as the true believers, the chosen, the favored ones. The Holy Spirit, however, honors no such distinctions. The Spirit welcomes all into the Kingdom, as we read in the account from Acts.

Such chauvinism is not limited to religion, however. We like to extend it to nationalities as well. Think of what our reaction is when we read in the newspaper about a plane being hijacked somewhere in the world. Isn't one of our first concerns whether there are any Americans on board? The hijacking is much more serious if American lives are at stake. That's a distinction we make: American lives are more valuable than other human lives. But God doesn't make that distinction. In Christ there is no Jew or Greek. God doesn't see some nationalities as more important than others. God makes no such distinction among persons.

During the U.S. invasion of Panama a few years ago, the news accounts of the casualties inflicted by the fighting spoke mostly of the U.S. soldiers and citizens who were killed or injured. Only once in a while was mention made of the Panamanian casualties. To this day, I understand, there is still no accurate report of the total number of Panamanians killed or wounded. We want to distinguish between Panamanian and American casualties. We want to emphasize American losses as more important. But God doesn't make that distinction.

Probably a good number of us have a U.S. passport. It's a valuable thing to have: It proves our citizenship. It allows us to travel freely into many countries in the world, and gives us some measure of protection if we get into difficulty or trouble. We have, however, a document that's far more important than a passport: our baptismal certificate. The fact of being baptized in Christ is infinitely more important than being a citizen of the United States or any other nation. Through baptism, one becomes a member of the people of God, a worldwide family that recognizes no distinctions of race or nationality or status or importance. The Spirit is given to all of us. The Spirit embraces all nations, all peoples. We humans are the ones who create the differences that cause war and hatred and cruelty. We humans are the ones who try to claim the Spirit as belonging to our group alone.

Our divisive thinking creates differences that do not exist in nature. Racism, for example, has been the cause of terrible violence and discrimination throughout human history. Yet scientific evidence now indicates that race is an artificial distinction. In an editorial a few years ago, Joan Beck of the *Chicago Tribune* wrote about this. She quoted Leonard Lieberman, a professor of anthropology at a Midwestern university, who says, "Race as a scientific concept is being abandoned. A majority of anthropologists no longer support the race concept."

Anthropologists and other scientists once thought that they could identify racial differences scientifically. Over decades, they developed thousands of measurements in an attempt to come up with racial classifications. But they failed to find the reliable, consistent evidence to prove racial differences, even on a genetic level. The more physical attributes they examined, the more difficult it became to find racial patterns and clear divisions separating them. For example, obvious traits such as skin color or hair color vary so much and are distributed in such uneven patterns that they are useless as scientific criteria.[1]

The upshot of all this research is that it has proven to be scientifically impossible to construct a viable theory of race. In other words, racial differences can't be found in nature. Of course, there are superficial differences among peoples, but nothing that would support a theory of race. Race is a concept that our exclusive thinking imposes on reality. Racism is a product of our fear, our need to elevate our group above others so that our group can secure what it wants. Centuries of bigotry, violence, and even genocide have been perpetuated simply by an idea conjured up in our minds. In reality, there are no divisions among people. All divisive distinctions are artificial creations of our thinking.

Suppose I were to wake up one morning and find myself in a field in the middle of a dense forest, without knowing how I got there. I look all around and see nothing but dark forest surrounding me. In panic, I decide that the forest is an impenetrable wall, and that I'm trapped. And so I remain in the middle of the field, paralyzed by my false belief. In fact, the forest is full of fascinating vegetation and wildlife, but I'm never able to see it because I think I'm confined to the field. I'm free to wander anywhere, but my thoughts have built a cage around me.

The distinctions and classifications we make about people create a steel cage for us. We're not free to enjoy the life that is possible for us as a human family.

In a family, when there is a rift between mother and son, or between brother and sister, the entire family is harmed. Every member of the family is affected by that breakup. Today, all of us suffer whenever there are conflicts or subjugation in the human family. Every one of us is affected. Martin Luther King, Jr., once said about his civil rights work: "We have to do this for the white people. As long as there is racism, it's the white people who aren't free." Whenever people are oppressed, all of us are confined to a prison of our own making.

In the passage cited from Acts, it wasn't a case of Peter and the early Christians having to recognize the equal right of the Gentiles to baptism. It wasn't a situation of "rights" that

needed to be honored. Rather, the early Christians discovered, through the prompting of the Spirit, that they needed
the Gentiles for their own healing and wholeness. As long as
the Gentiles were excluded, the Spirit was excluded. The
Christian community, and indeed the human family, is not
complete until all are included.

The idea that some must be excluded is always a product
of our flimsy thinking. Let us be willing to see this, and to see
the reality of our unity in Christ. Let us allow the Spirit, who
embraces all peoples, to enlighten our understanding.

18

The Ripple Effect

~

There's a story about a group of people in a small boat, out in the middle of the ocean. One of the passengers in the boat began to carve a hole in the bottom of the vessel, underneath where he was seated. His neighbors in the boat shrieked, "What are you doing? You'll drown us all!" The man retorted, "What I'm doing is none of your business. I paid my fare for this boat trip, so I'm entitled to do what I please. After all, I'm only making a hole below where I'm sitting."

It's a falsehood to think that how we live doesn't have an impact on the rest of the planet; that life is purely a matter of my individual preference, and that it's nobody else's business. And yet this view is commonly held today.

The book *Habits of the Heart: Individualism and Commitment in American Life*, by Robert Bellah and others, describes how individualism has become so pronounced in our American way of life that the very well-being of our nation is at risk. We often have little sense of community beyond our own family. We become concerned about political issues and world affairs when they might touch our family or our finances, but otherwise we can be largely indifferent. "If it doesn't affect my household, it's not my concern" is a prevalent attitude today. We can see government and politics as a dirty game, from which we prefer to keep our distance. Our home is our private enclosure. We venture outside to earn our livelihood, but getting the paycheck can be more important than having a job that is actually contributing to the common good. We keep to ourselves, and we expect our neighbors to do the same. Everyone minds his or her own business.

How can we hope to solve the serious problems facing our world and our nation today when we live with this sense of isolation? We can't. Our survival as a democratic people is jeopardized by this extreme individualism.

The Trappist monk Thomas Merton was a hermit. He lived a good part of his monastic life in a small hut some distance away from the rest of his brother monks, who remained in the monastery. But he had such a deep, prayerful concern about what was going on in the monastery and in the rest of the world that he had a powerful effect on countless people. His essays and books of spirituality touched many people's lives. And despite the fact that he died over twenty-five years ago, his books remain popular today. Thomas Merton showed that even a hermit can have an enormous impact on other people.

What we do, how we live, always has an effect on others. Even the little things are important. If I'm impatient with the traffic as I drive into town, honking my horn and trying to get ahead, I add a little more frustration to the world. The other drivers who felt my impatience may react by taking out their frustration on still other drivers, or on their families. If, instead of being so impatient, we're gentle in the way we drive, we can be a healing presence to those who come near us.

The way I speak to my spouse, the care and attention with

which I do my job, the greeting I give to my neighbor—it all has a ripple effect. At every moment, we are having an impact on our human environment.

Recently, I went to an acupuncturist because of a problem in my left knee. I was having some pain and stiffness that may have been the result of an old injury. Traditional medical remedies weren't working, so I wanted to try something else. When the acupuncturist inserted the needles, I was surprised that he placed them all in the right side of my body, even in my right foot! I asked him, "Are you sure this is going to help my left knee?" He just nodded. The results were remarkable. The pain began to subside after only a few treatments. Though the pain had been in my left knee, the problem was solved when the acupuncturist unblocked energy or healing chemicals in other parts of the body—which indicates that the body is not a jumble of disconnected parts, but an organic whole.

Likewise, as members of the Body of Christ, we form a living whole: We are all affected by one another's pain or distress, joy or peace.

Mystics have known for centuries that creation is one, that the whole universe can be seen within even a tiny pebble. The Zen patriarch Dogen said, "One has to accept that in this world there are millions of objects and that each one is, respectively, the entire world... [E]very object, every living thing is the whole...."[1] Walt Whitman said, "I believe a leaf of grass is no less than the journey-work of the stars..." and "I am large, I contain multitudes."[2] Science, especially quantum physics, is beginning to confirm the oneness of everything.[3] Science is discovering that the physical world we see is in fact a vast field of fluid energy. We are not disconnected blobs of matter. Matter, in fact, is just a form of energy. Everything shares in creation's energy.

The teaching about the Real Presence of Christ in the

Eucharist is, in a way, a reflection of this same truth. The cosmic Christ can be truly present in even a small piece of bread because in the universe nothing is separate; no one is isolated. Each particle contains all. We are all linked; we are all part of the mystical Body. The Eucharist isn't just about Christ's presence to us, although that's a major part of it. Christ is really present to us in and through the bread and the wine. But there's more to it than that. The Eucharist is also about us, about who we are. We who partake of the one bread are also one. We are the Body of Christ.

The Eucharist should forever lay to rest a widespread misconception in the way we live today: that it's every man for himself, or every woman for herself; that we have to "look out for Number One." In actuality, we are the Body. We are all joined. We do tremendous damage by thinking that we're not.

This unity also means that we have a responsibility to take care of our spiritual ecosystem. We know that putting chemical pollutants into the air or ocean can affect people on the other side of the globe. The same is true with our emotional or spiritual pollutants: hatred, bitterness, fear—these can spread and poison the human climate for everyone.

If I'm bitter, what I do with that bitterness is very important. If I can be completely aware of that feeling of bitterness, it will begin to disappear. It will evaporate under the flame of awareness. When I die to bitterness in this way, an energy is released that affects the whole Body. The Church used to call this "offering it up" for the salvation of the world or for the souls in purgatory. It still makes sense today. My act of dying to bitterness may help provide the grace, the strength, for someone on the other side of the planet to forgive a wrong done to him. We are that connected.

The way we handle our suffering is crucial. We tend to think suffering is meaningless, and therefore we use all manner of ways to avoid it: drugs, addictions, denial. All this increases our sense of misery and loneliness. If we can embrace our pain, however, a shift takes place. We discover that while we have pain, *we* are not the pain. "I'm feeling despair, but I am not the despair. It's OK." When we can be with our pain in this way, we feel the suffering of the world. We become one with suffering people everywhere. We realize that everyone is somehow in pain, and that we are united with them. We become compassion, and we experience healing. Our compassion can help release the energy for others, near and far, to find healing in their own suffering.

In every instant of our lives, we are contributing something to the spiritual climate of the world. We are not freestanding entities. There's always an energy being emitted from our smokestack. Is it pure flame, or polluted smoke? The good news about this is that no matter what our life may have been in the past, we can change. We can begin to live mindfully. We can be life-giving.

When we embrace the circumstances of our life at every moment, we are the Body that makes up what Saint Paul says was lacking in the Passion of Christ. We contribute to the salvation of the world. The Eucharist gives us the strength to do this, to be what we already are: the mystical Body of Christ.

19

Present-Moment Living

~

For many of us today, life isn't as good as we hoped it would be. Life is hard. Maybe we work long hours in a job we don't like. Perhaps we've been hit with a serious illness, or the trauma of a divorce. We may have suffered the tragic death of a loved one. "Where is God?" we ask.

All of this is the experience of the void, the absence of God. But the truth is that the void is not a void. God is not absent—we only feel that way. Jesus' disciples had that same feeling of absence after the Ascension (Acts 1:8-11). What were they to do, now that he had left? How could they manage without the one who had given them such powerful leadership and inspiration? To whom could they now turn for guidance and direction? They felt lost. And so they stood there, gazing up into the sky.

Jesus' departure wasn't really an absence, however. The Ascension anticipated Pentecost, when the disciples would receive the power of the Holy Spirit. The Spirit would be God's continuing presence to the world.

Jesus' Ascension has a great deal to teach us today, when our world feels an apparent absence of God. Civilization seems to be in a downward spiral; there is a breakdown in morality.

The Church was once generally regarded as God's presence on earth, but there's widespread skepticism about that belief today. In recent years, the Church, through the misconduct of some of its people and ministers, has shown its human, unseemly side. Some people feel disillusioned by these events. They think God is absent.

But God is never absent. The Ascension is always linked to Pentecost. The Spirit is not just some hollow belief; the Spirit can be found in what's actually happening in our world and in our daily lives. Our task is to be real, to face our life as it is.

Recently, a bishop from the Midwest gave a retreat to the priests of my diocese. In one of his talks, he spoke about what he called the "massive shift" that is taking place in our world today. We're living in a time of enormous change and upheaval. "What is it all about?" he asked the priests. "Where is this shift taking us?" Many of us ask the same questions today. Where is our world headed?

Fr. Hugo Enomiya-Lassalle, the German Jesuit and Zen Master, provides, I think, part of the answer. In his book *Living in the New Consciousness*[1], he notes that it wasn't until the time of Plato that humans became conscious of clock time. Before then, people were aware of day and night, and even the phases of the moon, but they had no concept of minutes and hours as we have now. Today, our awareness of the clock and our concern about time have grown to the point where time is a serious problem for us. We're preoccupied with time. We feel burdened by our memories of the past, or we're anxious about the future. We live mostly in the past or the future, with all the accompanying stress-related illnesses: heart disorders, nervousness, cancer.

Fr. Lassalle says that human consciousness is now discovering the possibility of living in what he calls the "fourth dimension": a way of being that includes freedom from time. This doesn't mean that we would throw away all our clocks and watches (though we might get rid of some of them!). It means that we would be free of our psychological fixation on time. In the fourth dimension, time is no longer a threat, a worry, or a problem for us. We come upon this freedom when we live fully in the present moment.

In my experience, present-moment living has tremendous appeal for people today. People find that it offers healing and liberation from the fear, worry, and guilt that plague them. I'm convinced that a major part of the massive shift that our world is experiencing today is a movement toward freedom from time.

There are some who have questions about this, though. When I give talks about meditation and the need for inner silence in our lives, people sometimes ask me, "What does all that have to do with Christ? How can we find God if we stop thinking about him? What does all this present-moment stuff have to do with the Christian faith?" The answer is this: Either Christ is real or he is not. Either Pentecost is real or it's not. If God is real, then the place to encounter God is in what's actually taking place from moment to moment, in life as it is at each moment. God is not a fleeting thought in our minds. God is the ineffable ground of everything that is. When we live with inner silence, we open ourselves to this Reality.[2]

People are rejecting empty belief today. A God who uses heaven and hell as a carrot and stick to keep us in line, or a God who is going to solve our problems and make all our dreams come true, just isn't genuine. It's a make-believe god.

The responsibility of the Church today is to be real. Quite frankly, the massive shift in the world today is going to render our Church irrelevant unless we are focused in reality. To be centered in reality means present-moment living.

Some months ago, I was taught a lesson in present-moment living. A very close friend of mine was killed in an automobile accident. I had never before faced the sudden loss of a friend like that, and it was a tremendously difficult experience. Feelings of grief came over me in waves. At this time of personal suffering, I found my meditation practice to be a source of great strength. The meditation allowed me to let the grief come up, without fighting it. I remember sitting in meditation with tears streaming down my face. This went on for days. I sat with the sadness, without trying to either resist it or prolong it. At times I felt as though I were riding a tidal wave of grief. I managed to do nothing to oppose it, and at a certain point I seemed to crest the worst of it. After that it began to subside.

Today I still feel my friend's physical absence—people are unique and irreplaceable—but the sadness is completely gone. I'm left with a deep sense of gratitude for having known him.

The Ascension shows that no person is indispensable to us. Not even the man Jesus of Nazareth was indispensable to the disciples. "If I do not go away, the Advocate will not come to you," Jesus told them (John 16:7). The Spirit gives us the power never to have to be a victim of our loss. When we can face our pain, our grief, or our disappointment, and experience it as it is, we find peace and healing.

Our challenge as Christians is to live in reality rather than try to avoid it. Fear of boredom, for instance, is a common problem today. We're so afraid of boredom that we do all we can to escape it. We try to keep constantly busy, amused, or entertained. Television, videos, video games, drugs, our preoccupation with sex—these are the means many people use to escape from emptiness. But what is boredom? Boredom, as

Jack Kornfield says, "comes from a lack of attention."[3] Boredom arises from our judgment that this moment isn't worth our full attention. Try this: The next time you find yourself feeling bored, don't run for the television or the telephone. Experience your boredom. Feel the physical sensations, the tension, the anxiousness, that make up your boredom. Don't resist it. If you stay with your boredom, you can find that no moment is really empty. The boredom will begin to evaporate. Just the sensations of breathing in and out can be marvelous if you stop to experience them.

Our troubles today stem largely from a failure to live the moment. Anger comes from our inability to be with the way things are. Greed, the desire for more and more, arises from our displeasure with the way our life is.

We think that life has to change in order for us to be happy. But, as many mystics have said, true happiness doesn't have a cause. True happiness doesn't have a reason. Happiness comes when we're able to live the moment. To face what is, to live the moment, is to find the Spirit's healing.

People today, especially Christians, are going through a collective dark night of the soul. They find themselves less and less able to hold on to images of an unreal God, a God who demands that we dwell on the sins of the past or the rewards or punishment of the future. Those idols are being abandoned. Once the traditional images and idols are discarded, what's left? What's left is the void, the seeming absence of God. What's left is our life as it is, with all the struggle and difficulty that go with it. The Christian life is about discovering that God is not absent in any of this, that God is powerfully present, even in this experience of the barren desert. In fact, our desert experiences of suffering and loss and emptiness are necessary for union with God. They strip us of our defensive barriers, and allow us to surrender to this fully real God.

Jesus says to us, just as he said to Mary Magdalene, "Do not hold on to me, because I have not yet ascended to the Father" (John 20:17). As Ascension people, we are left with this absence. We want to avoid the empty feeling, we want to cling to our myriad escapes from reality. All the while, we are like the apostles who stood there daydreaming, gazing up into the clouds. The disciples had to quit their daydreaming, and so must we. As people of Pentecost, we are to be open to encountering the Spirit in the one place where the Spirit is always to be found: in each present moment.

20

Listening to the Inner Voice

~

T he importance of listening to our inner voice is illustrated by the story of Samuel (1 Samuel 3:3-10,19). The Book of Samuel is the story of a young man who came to realize he had a prophetic call. It wasn't an easy discovery for him. After all, Samuel was merely a priest's assistant. He didn't expect to hear the Lord's voice. He didn't know what to make of it when he did hear it. What's more, "The word of the LORD was rare in those days" (3:1). There weren't many prophets then. Samuel had no role models to learn from. He was on his own with this inner voice.

And so when he heard the call, the voice that came to him in the stillness of his sleep, Samuel was confused. He thought it might be the voice of his mentor, Eli the priest. He made this mistake three times before Eli finally gave him permission to trust the voice. Once Samuel began to trust the voice, "the Lord was with him," not permitting any word of his to be without effect. In fact, Samuel's inner voice revealed to him some unsettling things. He learned that the sons of his mentor, Eli, had blasphemed the Lord, and that Eli's household faced hard times as a result. Samuel had to relate this difficult news to Eli (3:11-18). Samuel, the Scripture tells us, became a "trustworthy prophet of the LORD" (3:20).

A prophet tells the truth, speaks the Word of God, in situations where the truth is being ignored or stifled because of fear, greed, or injustice. A prophet is so attuned to that inner voice that he or she is not afraid to proclaim that truth, even though it may make other people upset or angry.

Abraham Heschel, the Jewish scholar who wrote a classic two-volume study of the prophets, says that there is an element of the prophet in every human being. Every one of us has that prophetic voice, deep within us. But are we listening to it? We hear this voice only when we listen out of an inner silence. We have to hear as did Samuel, whose only prayer was, "Speak, Lord, for your servant is listening."

Silence is something of a rarity in our world today. We constantly seek entertainment and amusement and noise to stifle our boredom. Even more, we destroy silence by our own internal noise. We find it hard to speak the truth because other inner voices overwhelm it. How many of us can say something that we know we need to say, but that might cause our spouse, our children, or our friends to be displeased with us? How many of us can take a stand on something that we know will cause us to be disapproved of by the group to which we belong?

Often, we can be too afraid to speak the truth because we're worried about protecting our position. We want to be liked, we want others to be pleased with us, we fear rejection. We want to be right, we want to preserve our reputation. If we look bad, if we're proved wrong about something, if someone has hurt us, we feel insignificant. We're terribly afraid of being insignificant.

And so we protect our position. We say things that aren't true, or we shade the truth so that others will continue to like us or look up to us. Or we lash out in anger at someone who has hurt us. The upshot of all this is that the Word of the Lord is rarely heard today, just as was the case in Samuel's day. Our own noise drowns out the truth. So, like Samuel, we have to listen and listen and listen, so that the noise may begin to fade.

Let's say we have an argument with someone—our spouse, a member of our family, somebody at work. We both feel strongly about the matter. We have a heated exchange, but it doesn't resolve anything. We both speak out of our noise. We judge each other to be wrong. We hurt each other by what we say, or by our attitude or tone of voice. In the end, the argument only creates distance between us. We haven't discussed or settled anything. We've simply protected our position.

Arguments are often painful, but they can actually be a fruitful opportunity to get in touch with our inner silence. Like Samuel, we have to have the patience to listen, to wait. During the argument, we're upset, we feel that this other person is a dimwit, we know we're right. Can we simply be with all of that din and wait for it to settle? As long as we're controlled by our anger, anything we say will be hurtful or manipulative.

There's a verse from the ancient *Tao Te Ching* that says, "Do you have the patience to wait until your mind settles and the water is clear? Can you remain unmoving until the right action arises by itself?" Do we have the forbearance to wait until the storm created by our argument is over? The Zen Master Joko Beck shares some real wisdom here:

> The right words will say themselves if we have
> settled down. We can't do this without sin-
> cere practice. It may not be a formal prac-
> tice; sometimes we just take a deep breath,
> wait for a second, feel our guts, and then
> speak. On the other hand, if we're having a
> major conflict with somebody, we may need
> more time. It might be better to say nothing
> for a month.[1]

Jesus told his disciples that they were going to face some
very difficult situations, but he counseled them, "Do not worry
about how you are to speak or what you are to say; for what
you are to say will be given to you at that time…" (Matthew
10:19). The Christian life is about having faith that what we
need to say and what we need to do will be given to us, provided we have the patience to wait for the storm to subside.

If we can stay with our inner clamor, we will find that the
waiting and listening constitute a healing process. They heal
us of our need to protect our position. In my own life, I have
found that the experience of being hurt can be a powerful
occasion for listening. When someone hurts us, we feel as if
we are nothing, as if we have been rendered totally unimpor-
tant. We're terrified of that feeling. We become angry almost
automatically. Anger is a way of assuring ourselves that we
are still somebody to be reckoned with. Do we have the patience to keep quiet and to remain with the feeling of being
nothing, to be with the anger and the confusion that come
from being hurt? I don't like feeling hurt, and I'm uncomfortable with the pain and the emptiness it brings. None of us
likes to feel stepped-on and insignificant. But this experience
of being nothing is silence. In that silence, we can come upon
what to say and how to say it, what to do, and what not to do,

in response to someone who has hurt us. We come upon the truth that needs to be spoken. Nothingness is where we can find the prophetic voice within us: "Speak, Lord, for your servant is listening." In that quiet listening, we begin to realize that there is nothing about us that we need to protect.

Our prophetic call means that we must be listening every day, staying with our thoughts and emotions every day, just allowing them to be, waiting for the insight that comes from inner stillness.

The Benedictine monk Brother David Steindl-Rast says, "All real words come out of silence and lead you into silence." There are no true words without silence. Imagine a room filled with fifty radios, each one tuned to a different channel, each with the volume turned on high. The noise would be so garbled and deafening that nothing intelligible could be heard. Without silence, words have no meaning. Our life can be like that radio room. Life lacks meaning for people today because there's no silence. All we can hear is the garbled cacophony of our self-protective noise. We fear being hurt by others; we react defensively to others; we judge others. We don't communicate. Only inner stillness can heal our suffering.

We alone are responsible for the prophetic voice within us. In a real way, we are on our own with that inner voice. No one can do our listening for us. Like Samuel, who tried to lean on Eli, we want someone else to give us the answers, to take away the pain and confusion of our life. But only we can face our life as it is. Only we can discover the quiet that's underneath our inner chatter. I'm convinced that this requires a daily practice of silent prayer. Breathing Prayer and Centering Prayer are two possibilities. (See Appendix II.) It is important that we have some prayer that allows us to remain unmoving in the midst of our inner clamor, a prayer that helps us to wait for insight in the center of our confusion.

If the word of the Lord is rare today, it's because we're not listening. If we are to hear the truth and speak it, our attitude must be that of Samuel, who grew quiet in the presence of the Lord, waiting to hear the Lord's voice.

21

The God of the Now

~

Our past can be an oppressive weight upon us. One of the biggest blocks to experiencing our ever-present God is guilt: the guilt trips we lay on ourselves because of the mistakes we've made, the hurtful things we've done. Guilt can keep us living in the past. "That was a terrible thing I did; I'll never be able to forget it." "I'm a really awful person to have done such a hurtful thing." We can continually put ourselves down and dwell in the past. And so we never experience the God who says, "What's past is past; live in the present moment, where I am with you, trying to share my life with you."

After the arrest of John the Baptist, Jesus tried to exhort people to live in the present moment. He announced that the time for waiting was ended. "This is the time of fulfillment. The kingdom of God is at hand! Repent, and believe in the gospel" (Mark 1:15, *New American Bible* translation).

For centuries, the Israelites had waited and hoped for the day when God would act decisively and end their misery. With the announcement made in Mark's Gospel, Jesus meant to put an end to all of that anticipation. What the Israelites had long been hoping for was now upon them. God's decisive reign was in their midst. It was here, it was now. They had only to live accordingly.

For many people in Jesus' day, this message didn't sink in. They couldn't believe that God's reign had truly arrived in their own lives. Jesus had to be mistaken, they thought.

We too can have a hard time believing what Jesus said. The Kingdom is here at this moment in your life, in my life. But the fact is that we miss this presence of God because we're burdened by the weight of the past, or preoccupied with our wants and worries for the future. If we really knew that God's reign is here, our lives would be different.

Jesus' words in the gospel tell us something very important about God. God lives and acts in the here and now. God doesn't dwell in the past. God isn't some unfulfilled promise of the future. God is here, at this moment.

There's a story from the Middle Ages about a nun who claimed that she had a vision of Christ. The bishop asked, "Sister, did you talk to him?"

And she said, "Yes, I did."

He continued, "If you have another vision, ask Christ this question: 'What was the bishop's great sin before he became a bishop?'" He knew that only God and his own confessor would know.

About three months later, the nun made an appointment to see the bishop. When she came in, he said, "Did you see our Lord again?"

"Yes," she replied.

"Did you ask him the question about my sin?"

"Yes, I did," she responded.

"And what did he say?"

She smiled and answered, "The Lord said, 'I don't remember anymore.' "[1]

Our God of unconditional love lives only in the now. To the extent that we can't forget our sins, we fail to experience this loving God.

I remember a professor who taught theology at my seminary. This professor, who was a psychiatrist and a theologian, had done an in-depth study of the notion of "guilt" in the Bible. What he concluded from his study was that there is only one purpose to guilt, and that purpose is self-knowledge.

If I blow up in a blinding rage every time someone criticizes me, and then later I feel sad about that, my feeling isn't meant to tell me that I'm a bad person. No, that guilt can help to teach me something about myself. It raises a red flag; it tells me that there is some deep-seated fear or anger in my life that I seriously need to look at so that I don't continue to hurt people.

God wants us to grow, not to feel bad about ourselves. God wants conversion, not guilt trips. So often the word "guilt" is equated with self-hatred. We hate ourselves for the wrong we've done. But self-intolerance inhibits the growth and freedom to which God calls us. A better term that we can substitute for guilt is "responsibility." If I do something hurtful, then I have a responsibility to learn from that experience, and I have a responsibility to repair any damage that I've done. But I can do so without any guilt trips, because it accomplishes nothing to feel bad about myself. We are always accepted by our God of unconditional love, and it does us no good to deny that.

It is not easy for us to live this gospel truth, however. We seem to go through life as if we're carrying a Polaroid Camera, which we use to define our world. At some point in our lives, perhaps early on, we take a photograph of ourselves. It probably isn't a very flattering picture. We did something wrong, our parents told us that we were bad, or something hurtful or embarrassing happened to us, and snap!—we take the picture. That picture, that experience, is who we are—or so we're convinced. As the years go by, every bad thing we do, every failure, simply reaffirms for us the accuracy of that original photo.

What we may not realize is that we shoot our Polaroid Camera at other people too. Early on in our relationship with people, perhaps in our very first encounter with them, we snap the picture. Maybe it's a pleasant picture ("She's a nice person"), maybe it's not ("He's irritating"). But from that time on, that picture tends to define our relationship with the person. Even if we later change our opinion about a person, we simply take another snapshot of him or her. We relate to the person on the basis of this most recent photo. The picture is who that individual is, or so we think.

And so instead of living in reality, we spend our life gazing at our photo album. Instead of living in the here and now, we dwell on images from the past. And we try to relate to God in the same way.

God, however, lives only in the now. God looks at us afresh, at every moment, without an image. As a saint once said, "God is closer to us than we are to ourselves." God doesn't need a Polaroid Camera because God sees us as we are, at every moment. Our life may have been a complete mess for the past fifty years, but like the father of the prodigal son, God forgets all of that the instant we turn back to God. God doesn't need a photo album. God dwells only in the now, with no lingering images from the past. And God asks us to do the same.

Jesus' proclamation that the Kingdom is here is a summons to all of us to live in the present moment, where God is to be found. Helen Mallicoat writes beautifully about this in a meditation on the divine name:

> I was regretting the past
> and fearing the future.
> Suddenly my Lord was speaking:
> "My name is I AM." He paused.
> I waited. He continued.
> "When you live in the past,
> with its mistakes and regrets,
> it is hard. I am not there.
> My name is not *I Was*.
> When you live in the future,
> with its problems and fears,
> it is hard. I am not there.
> My name is not *I Will Be*.
> When you live in this moment,
> it is not hard. I am here.
> My name is *I AM*.[2]

22

The Real Miracle

~

M iracles hold great power to fascinate and con-
vert people. So why is it Jesus told those whom
he had cured to keep quiet about their
miracle? A leper is healed, a deaf man has his hearing re-
stored—why would Jesus want to keep such wonderful things
a secret? Part of the reason is hinted at in Mark 1:40-45: The
leper spread the story everywhere, and as a result of this, it
was no longer possible for Jesus "to go into a town openly."
In other words, everybody wanted to be cured. But Jesus'
mission wasn't to see to it that the whole human race was
physically cured. When Jesus was mobbed by people who
wanted some malady healed, they couldn't hear his real
message: that the Kingdom of God was at hand. The healing
miracles were a sign, a powerful sign, of God's Kingdom at
work. But the arrival of the Kingdom didn't mean that
everyone was going to be physically healed. It did not mean
that, from now on, everyone was entitled to a pain-free,
comfortable life. Jesus wanted to avoid giving people such
false ideas about his gospel message. And so, he tried, unsuc-

cessfully, to keep the news of the healing miracles from being spread.

There are people today, Christian and non-Christian, who seem to have an authentic gift for healing others. Through prayer, laying on of hands, or some other kind of touch, they are able to help people be cured of physical ailments. A couple of years ago, a famous Catholic priest with a healing ministry came to my town and conducted a large healing service attended by hundreds of people. Such healers, who apparently have a genuine gift, are widely sought after. We can be enthralled by the miracles that seem to be worked through them. We can see them as the answer to our pain, our suffering.

I can personally testify that this kind of physical healing takes place. Years ago, I experienced a physical healing of my own at a charismatic prayer service. It's a wonderful thing. But the Kingdom isn't a guarantee of our physical well-being.

Jesus' miracles were a sign that God cares—and cares deeply—about us. They were signs of the transformation that God offers us. God wants wholeness for us and for the entire human family. But fundamentally our wholeness means that we're able to experience the Kingdom even when life is tough. Fullness of life means that we can find joy even when life is painful. To live with that kind of wholeness is to be transformed. That's the real miracle Jesus was trying to bring about for people.

Like many of the people in Jesus' day, we too can miss the boat as to what the Kingdom is about. We can think that we're entitled to be comfortable.

Some time ago, I attended a Zen retreat (sesshin). On that retreat, I came face to face with my own need for comfort. During the retreat, we sat in the lotus (or semilotus) position for as many as eight or nine hours over the course of each day. Your knees become quite painful when you sit for that long!

At first, the pain was a terrible struggle for me. I couldn't bear it. I had to move, change positions, try to alleviate the aches and stiffness. But as the retreat progressed, I began to realize that the pain in my knees wasn't the real problem. The real problem was my reaction to the pain. "This is awful!" I kept thinking. "I can't go on! How am I going to have the stamina to sit tomorrow if I wear out my knees today?" My *fear* of the pain was the real cause of my trouble. When I realized that, I was able to just be with the pain, without resisting it. Instead of reacting to the pain, I started to notice all the sensations in my knees that made up the pain: the tenseness, the tingling, the tightness. As I observed all of its different aspects, the pain even became interesting! I was able to sit for longer and longer periods in peaceful meditation, without moving. It wasn't that my tolerance for pain had increased. I had simply dropped my fear of the pain, and so the pain was no longer such a big problem.

Life does not owe us a pleasant existence. We want comfort, we want everything to be nice and pleasing. When we're not feeling fine, when things are not going our way, when we're uncomfortable, we're not happy. We look for someone, maybe a new spouse or a new partner, to take the pain away. We search for some solution, some new life that promises us relief. We want Jesus to take away our suffering. But Jesus says, "The Kingdom is here," even in our distress. We can find happiness even in the midst of our pain.

There's a story about a woman who struggled with suffering. She was confined to a wheelchair as the result of a debilitating disease. For years and years, it was her dream to go to Lourdes, where she felt she would be cured. She longed for the miracle that would enable her to walk again. One night she had a dream. She dreamed that she was in her wheelchair, and Jesus walked up and embraced her. She felt tremendous healing and compassion in his touch. She wept tears of release, tears of joy. A few days later, her son came to visit her. He was surprised at the serene expression on her face as she sat in her wheelchair. She smiled and said, "It's OK, I don't need to go to Lourdes anymore. It's OK." That woman shows us the real miracle: to discover joy no matter what our circumstances.

There's an old Sufi tale about a seeker who traveled about the world looking to find the true God. He examined all religions and all communities in hopes of finding the perfect manifestation of God in life. In one of his trips, he stopped at a monastery and said to a monk, "Tell me, does your God work miracles?" The monk replied, "Well, it all depends on how you define a miracle. Some people think that it is a miracle if God does the will of people. But here in this community we think it is a miracle when people do the will of God."

Each one of us faces difficulties in life—trying circumstances, unpleasant things. Sometimes, at least, we can do nothing about these situations. We have no choice but to face the pain and the anguish, to live with it. When we are willing to face our life as it is, at every moment, we experience true healing. When we live our life as it is, from moment to moment, then our life is "Your will be done." When our life is "Your will," instead of an endless pursuit of our own comfort, we find fullness and joy. Isn't that the most important kind of healing there is?

This is no easy process for us. It means that we must always be willing to live in the here and now. Anytime we're upset, anytime we're distraught about something, that's a signal that we're not living in the here and now. The next time you're upset, notice what happens. You've taken yourself out of the present moment. We all do this when we're upset. We're thinking, "Things shouldn't be this way! Life shouldn't be like this!"

We cause ourselves so much unhappiness as a result. Our healing begins when we can be with our upset as we would an interesting twinge in the knee. This is hard to do, since we usually feel we're entitled to our upset. "I have a right to be mad about this!" we tell ourselves indignantly. But when we're distraught, we generally make a mess of things. Haven't we all done this? We don't respond appropriately to events and circumstances when we're distressed. And we miss the miracle of life. Are we willing to be with our upset, for as long as it lasts, instead of allowing it to control us? The more we can be with it, the more perceptive we will become about the right action we need to take to address the situation.

Jesus wanted the cures kept quiet because people were quick to conclude that the miracle would be easy and painless. Jesus didn't want people running around the countryside shouting about something they didn't truly understand. He asks us too to be quiet with what's actually happening in our life: our troubles, our worries, our suffering. In that stillness, we can encounter his compassionate touch. In the everyday circumstances of our life, we find the true source of our happiness.

23

The Sunday Bargain

~

J esus spoke in parables to the multitudes of ancient
Palestine. His audience consisted mainly of Jews,
descendants of nomads who had settled in Palestine centuries before. These people were used to being treated
like the doormat of the Middle East. Their land lay directly
in the path of a major trade route, and was a tempting target
for any foreign army. They were pillaged and conquered in
the eighth century B.C.E. by the Assyrians, and in the sixth
century B.C.E. by the Babylonians. Jews were uprooted and
exiled from their homeland on both occasions. During Jesus'
time, they were under Roman domination.

Many of the people of ancient Palestine were dirt-poor
peasants who would never have a hope of becoming wealthy
or powerful. They eked out a living as laborers or field hands,
in the withering heat of the Mideast sun. If any people in the
ancient world were entitled to have an inferiority complex,
they were. The women of their group were even worse off,
being regarded as little more than chattel by the men.

It was to these lowly, down-and-out people that Jesus addressed his beautiful parables about the reign of God in Mark 4:26-32. The reign of God, he said, is like a seed that is scattered and grows into ripe wheat, or like a tiny mustard seed that bursts to become a home for the birds of the sky. Jesus was speaking a marvelous message to the crowds: "The reign of God is about your growth. God wants you to grow, to attain fullness of life."

Fullness was God's gift and hope for the lowly Israelites, and it is God's wonderful plan for us as well. God has peace and joy in mind for us, and will settle for nothing less. Like the Israelites, however, we may have trouble believing that God intends such surprising gifts for this seemingly meager life of ours.

Two things are required of us if we are to cooperate with God's offer of boundless life: courage and patience.

We need courage to undergo the powerful change that God can work in us. We have to be willing to give up the need to have our life remain a certain way. The role of the Church, and how we see its role in our lives, is especially important here.

In Dostoyevsky's *The Brothers Karamazov*, there is a great scene in which Christ returns to earth, to Seville, Spain, in the midst of the Inquisition. The Grand Inquisitor has just burned a hundred heretics at the stake, and now Jesus comes, bringing healing and compassion. Everyone recognizes Jesus, but the Grand Inquisitor has him arrested and imprisoned. He tells Jesus (*I'm paraphrasing*), "We won't allow you to speak to the people. You see, we don't need you anymore. You gave the people freedom, but they don't want it. Freedom only makes them troubled and anxious. Instead, they want contentment. So they've given up their freedom, and in return we've given them authority and miracles, which make them feel content."

How do we see the Church today? Do we look to it for authority and miracles, or for freedom? The Church is not a crutch. The Church is, or should be, about helping people to grow, to point them toward fullness of life. But growth can be scary. A seed must die in order to yield ripe wheat. Our growth requires that we give up having to preserve our life as we know it, that we consent to a total transformation. That can be an intimidating prospect.

In our fear, we can turn to the Church as our security blanket. We want Church authority to assure us that we're safe. We want miracles that will captivate us. The result of all of this is the "Sunday Bargain." It's an unconscious arrangement that exists these days between the clergy and the people in the pews. The bargain is this: The clergy are to provide a Sunday service that is entertaining, or affirming, or leaves people with a good feeling, or at least assures them that all is well (or can be, if they behave themselves) between them and God. In return, the people are to attend the Sunday service, contribute to the collection, and be nice to the pastor. Both sides receive a payoff in this agreement. The Church receives financial support, and its clergy are treated well, while the people are made to feel good, or are assured of their reward in the hereafter. But nobody grows.

This subtle understanding is all too prevalent in the Christian Church today. Catholic and Protestant clergy alike have told me that it's something they struggle with.

One of the greatest hindrances to growth for Christians today is this Sunday Bargain. We have to acknowledge that this bargain exists, and the danger that it poses. We have to face the fear that gives rise to it. We have to be willing to live the gospel truth: that we find life not by preserving it, but by losing it.

The second thing required of us if we are to cooperate with

God's plan for our life is patience. Change doesn't happen overnight. Probably all of us have wrestled with something in our life, a fear or a hang-up, and after a while we thought we'd finally outgrown it, only to learn that it's still with us. We need to realize that growth doesn't take place in a neat progression. It's more like an upward spiral: We keep returning to the same issues in our life, but each time at a higher level of maturity. When we notice the recurrence of a fear we've been grappling with for years, we may be disappointed to discover that we haven't outgrown it. Yet in fact we're now looking at our fear with greater understanding, and more freedom than we had before.

Transformation takes place gradually. Just as the farmer goes to bed and gets up day after day, while the seed sprouts and grows, change occurs within us without our realizing that it's happening. We recognize growth only after it has occurred. It's not our accomplishment. It's the work of the reign of God. We can only keep the ground fertile by paying attention to our thoughts and emotions. When we stay with our fear, and stay with it, and stay with it, slowly, over time, it loses its grip over us. One day we look and notice a freedom within us that we never knew before. What's happened is that we've lost something of the life we've known but gained something eternal. This is how it is, Jesus tells us, in the reign of God.

Many of the people of Jesus' day had a hard time believing the Good News he preached. The prospect that their lives could be transformed was too much to comprehend, too daunting a task to consider. They lessened themselves by their lack of faith.

Today we diminish ourselves when we shy away from the journey of transformation. Both the institutional Church and the people in the pews bear responsibility for this.

The Church is nervous about the possibility that its people might be transformed. Over the centuries, the Christian mystical tradition has produced some powerful and integrated people, such as Saint John of the Cross and Saint Teresa of Avila. But the Church seems always to be threatened by such people. John of the Cross once came close to being excommunicated. Saint Teresa was harassed by her own community. Mystics are not subject to fear or guilt, and therefore can't be manipulated or controlled. They know firsthand the law of God in their heart, and have no use for psychological dependence on authority. The Church doesn't like to contend with such people.

Those in the pews also share responsibility here. It's easier to remain asleep than to be aware. There's a certain feeling of protection that comes from abdicating our life to some external power. But it's a false sense of safety, since it's founded on the desire to avoid what's actually happening in our lives.

Jesus said, "I came to bring fire to the earth" (Luke 12:49). So much of the activity of the Church today, including its liturgy and preaching, can be focused on affirming or entertaining people, or helping them to feel good. While these things may have their place, this emphasis lacks respect for the human person. People are capable of much more than having to be affirmed and stroked at every turn.

Jesus challenged people. He expected the most out of them. He did not coddle them. His attitude was: "You are extraordinary. Your life is to be set ablaze. You can be so free that you live without fear, without clinging to people or things. Like a grain of wheat that has died, you can be so transformed that you are life-giving to all. You can live with such tremendous inner peace that you are no longer even angry with your brother or sister. You can have life, and have it to the full."

The parables of the seed and the mustard shrub manifest the infinite respect that Jesus had for the people of his time, and that he continues to have for us today. We were created for magnificence, and creation will not rest until we discover that and live that. The question is: Do we respect ourselves enough to take these parables seriously?

24

"God Help Us If We Got What We Deserve!"

~

We don't have to look very far today to see the signs of human suffering. The starving children in Africa; the maimed victims of ethnic violence in Bosnia; the growing number of homeless and street people, of abused and neglected children in our nation; people living in fear of crime and violence in our cities. We see news reports of these things almost every day on television or in the newspaper.

"I am all of these suffering people," Jesus says. "As often as you did it for one of my least brothers or sisters, you did it for me."

The only solution to all of this human misery is the compassion of Christ. To have the compassion of Christ, we must see ourselves in the suffering people of the world.

There's a story about a man who was once an active member of the Ku Klux Klan. For him, people of the white race were the only valuable people. He looked on people of other races, especially blacks, as less than human. And he spread his hatred with a vengeance. He took part in all of the Klan rallies and cross burnings. He spread the Klan's hate-filled, racist literature through the mail and on the streets. And whenever they got the chance, he and his fellow Klansmen didn't hesitate to use physical violence against minorities. But one night this man had a dream. He dreamed he was holding a club and chasing a black man. He wanted to do terrible harm to this black man. He chased him for blocks and blocks, and finally he cornered the man in an alley. At that point in his dream, the Klansman lifted his club, grabbed hold of the black man, and spun him around so that they faced each other. But when he looked at the black man, he was dumbstruck to see that the man had his, the Klansman's, face; this man he had been chasing and wanting to kill had his own face!

And as he thought about the dream afterward, he began to realize that in all his racist hatred, it was first of all himself whom he had been hating, a part of himself that he couldn't accept.

That story is important to me because in my own life I have come to realize that my spiritual challenge is to see that there is a part of me that is black, a part of me whose skin is brown, red, yellow, and unless I accept that, love that, I will be the worst racist.

The answer to racism is not simply more laws or a media campaign to raise our consciousness about the harmfulness of bigotry. These things can help, but they are not the answer. The answer to racism is to see ourselves in people of other races. For to see that is to have the heart of Christ.

And how about the poor? How do we feel if we're standing on a corner next to a street person who hasn't had a bath in two weeks? Or the billion people living in poverty elsewhere

in the world—Haiti, Latin America, Asia—do we catch ourselves thinking, "Well, it's their own fault that they're poor
and hungry. If they only worked as hard as we do and used
their brains like we do, they wouldn't have it so bad"?

The late Dorothy Day spent much of her life working, as a
member of the Catholic Worker Movement, among the poor-
est of our poor in the slums of New York and elsewhere. A
number of years ago, she told about a small incident that happened while she was walking to her home one evening in
1948. Her home was on Mott Street. She said:

> It is always a terrible thing to come back to
> Mott Street. To come back in a driving rain
> to men crouched on the stairs, huddled in
> doorways, without overcoats because they
> sold their overcoats—perhaps the week be-
> fore when it was warm, to satisfy their hun-
> ger or thirst, who knows. *Those without love*
> would say, 'It serves them right drinking up
> their clothes, selling their clothes to buy
> booze, it serves them right.' But God help us
> if we got what we deserve![1]

If we take a long, honest look at our life, most of us will
have to admit that there's a part of us that's poor, that's not a
success, that doesn't measure up. What's more, there's a part
of us that's *unworthy* poor, a part of us that's a failure and has
no excuse for failing, no excuse.

In Saint Paul's First Letter to the Corinthians, he describes
what real love is: Love is patient, kind; love holds no grudges;
love rejoices only in the good, not the bad.... How many of
us live up to this standard of love, every day of our lives? Most
of us, at least, would have to admit that we fail at this. And

we have no excuse for our failure. This is just one example of how we are "unworthy" poor.

To the extent that I don't acknowledge and love that part of me that is "unworthy" poor, I deny the gospel, because God loves the unworthy poor in me, in you, in the suffering people of the world, with an infinite love. And God asks us to do the same.

Jesus didn't come to earth to tell us that God is with us only when we've got our act together. No, Jesus' message was that God is with us even though our life may be a mess. As a matter of fact, it's precisely in the midst of our mess, our failure, our sin, that God is with us.

It's almost as if our weakness is necessary, because God's grace can't touch us where we think we are strong. We won't allow God to reach us in our strength; we don't think we need any help where we're strong. It's in our weakness, in those parts of us we feel we must reject—it is precisely there—that God can touch us most powerfully. It is there that God can show us that we are one with all of the rejected and suffering people of the world. It is in our own weakness that we discover Christ's compassion for all people; it is when we see ourselves in other hurting people that we have the compassion of Christ.

Think about the people you dislike the most, especially the one whom you avoid like the plague. Can you look at that person and become him? Can you become her? Can you see his fear and insecurity; can you feel her pain? Can you see yourself in that person?

The refugee, terrorized and homeless, searching for some asylum; the powerful drug lord, driven by fear and greed; the child prostitute, wandering the streets with no hope—can we see all of them as our neighbor? Can we see that we *are* them?

Today's gospel is a call to all of us to go beyond the fear and judgments that separate us from the suffering people of the world, indeed all people of the world. To go beyond the fear of our own weakness, the judgments we make about our own and others' failure. It's an invitation to move beyond all of that and to encounter our oneness with the human family, to discover within ourselves the boundless compassion of Christ.

25

The Dark Night

~

The Kingdom of Heaven is like a wedding banquet, a great celebration. But if we're not ready for it, it will pass us by. The five foolish bridesmaids weren't prepared for it (Matthew 25:1-13). They didn't have enough oil to keep their torches burning, and so they weren't around to celebrate when the groom arrived.

An important point of "being ready," this gospel passage tells us, is that we have to be prepared to endure a long vigil, a dark night, without knowing when it will end.

What is a "dark night"? It's an experience of deep suffering, pain, doubt, anguish, or abandonment that lasts and lasts, to the point where we wonder if it will ever come to an end. If we want to enter into communion with God, if we want a seat at the banquet, we're all going to have to go through one, perhaps more than once in our lifetime.

The effects of these painful events may linger in our lives for months and even years. We feel as if the rug has been completely pulled out from underneath us. And we don't know where to turn.

Some dark nights are mainly spiritual. The spiritual dark nights usually have no external cause. A spiritual dark night could involve, for example, an overwhelming sense that the deepest hopes, plans, and expectations that I had for my life have all been crushed.

Conventional wisdom tells us that we should try to avoid the dark night, escape it, or at least alleviate it. We should tranquilize ourselves or distract ourselves from it. Do anything but face it, so the thinking goes. But unless we face it, we're like those foolish bridesmaids who ran off and missed the Lord's arrival.

Some years ago, a young woman was involved in a terrible automobile accident. She was so badly injured that one of her legs had to be amputated. After she lost her leg, this once-energetic, athletic woman was reduced to a state of near-suicidal despair. She endured months of depression. Finally, after many such months, she decided to face her darkness. She began a program of painful rehabilitation and job retraining. She eventually took a job that involved counseling and helping to rehabilitate other people who had limbs amputated. She found joy in doing this new work, a joy that she had not known before. She was able to give a kind of help and support to amputees that other counselors couldn't.

Not too long ago, in an interview with a news reporter, this woman said, "If I had the choice to get my old life back, the life I had before the accident, I would refuse it. I've experienced so much happiness, so much fulfillment, in my new life that I would rather keep the life I have now." An amazing statement.

The gospel offers us new life, but we can't come upon this new life unless we keep vigil in the dark night. This is hard to do: I myself would rather not have to face the dark nights. I too find it hard to trust that these trying experiences can lead me to a deeper peace and union with God. It's a challenge for me and probably for every one of us.

Our normal reaction when we're confronted with a really agonizing period in our life is to question God: "How can you do this? How could you allow this to happen? Do something about it! Make things right again!" We want to force God to intervene and straighten out the situation. We fail to see how important the dark night can be for our own fullness of life.

There was a certain scientist who devoted his career to developing a strain of butterfly that would have the most beautiful blend of colors ever seen. After years of experimenting, he was sure that he had a cocoon that would produce his genetic masterpiece. On the day when the butterfly was expected to appear, he called together all of his staff. Everyone waited breathlessly as the butterfly began to work its way out of the cocoon. It withdrew its right wing, its body, and most of its left wing. Just as all the staff were ready to cheer and celebrate this great creation, they were shocked to see that the left wing of the butterfly was partially stuck in the cocoon. The insect was desperately flapping its right wing to free itself. This feverish struggle began to exhaust the butterfly. Each new effort seemed to take more energy out of the butterfly, and the intervals between efforts grew longer. Finally, the scientist, unable to bear the strain of watching, took a scalpel and cut a tiny section from the mouth of the cocoon. The butterfly made one final burst of effort and fell onto the laboratory table. Everybody cheered. Then they grew silent again, as they saw that, while the butterfly was free, it could not fly.[1]

The struggle to escape from the cocoon is necessary for the butterfly's proper development. It's Nature's way of forcing blood to the extremities of the butterfly's wings. Without this struggle, the butterfly will not develop the ability to fly. When the scientist tried to save the butterfly, he ruined its capacity to fly. He destroyed the freedom it was intended to have.

We want God to intervene in our dark night, but God can't intrude. Not without harming us.

The conventional wisdom tells us we should cope with the suffering that comes our way. We should do all we can to take our mind off it, take the pain and uncertainty away. We should try to find someone who can relieve our misery. Coping, however, only allows us to survive. It doesn't give us the marvelous freedom for which we were created.

The gospel isn't about our mere survival. It's not about coping, or just eking out an existence during our days on this planet. The gospel calls us to new life, a transformed life, where we are able to live fully in every circumstance, whether we're facing a time of abundance or a time of being brought low (Philippians 4:12-14).

To open ourselves to this new life means that we have to step into unknowing. We have to be willing not to understand the meaning or sense of it all. The Spanish mystic John of the Cross writes exquisitely about his own experience of this in his poem, "The Living Flame of Love":

> I entered into unknowing,
> yet when I saw myself there,
> without knowing where I was,
> I understood great things;
> I will not say what I felt
> for I remained in unknowing
> *transcending all knowledge.*
>
> That perfect knowledge
> was of peace and holiness
> held at no remove

in profound solitude;
it was something so secret
that I was left stammering,
transcending all knowledge....

Whoever truly arrives there
cuts free from himself;
all that he knew before
now seems worthless
and his knowledge soars
that he is left in unknowing
transcending all knowledge.[2]

We don't know where our suffering is taking us. That's perhaps the most difficult thing about the dark night. We don't have the foggiest idea where it's all leading. God uses the dark night to transform our life. If we are to arrive at wherever it is God is leading us, we have to accept our unknowing. Our need to know is perhaps the biggest barrier to God's work in our life. We want a solution, we want someone to give us the answer, but there is no answer. There's just us, in the dark night, feeling as though we're on our own.

We're not on our own, however, if we can face the darkness, if we don't grasp for false security. The Lord is near. The bridegroom will surely arrive, and then there will be cause for great celebration. Our life can be transformed in ways we never could imagine if we stay with it, if we keep watch through the night.

26

True Freedom

~

Today, when we think of "freedom," we often think of choice. To be "free" means having the right to choose where we will live, how we will live, what job we will take, the person we will marry, the beliefs we will hold, and so on. But freedom of choice is not freedom. Not really.

Let's say that I am addicted to drugs and alcohol. I wake up one morning and say to myself, "What am I going to get high on today? Today I choose drugs." I have exercised a choice here, but I'm certainly not free. My life is held captive by addiction.

We may not be hooked on drugs or alcohol, but our lives can be dominated by other escapes. We want comfort, relief from our anxiety and pain. We search for new amusements and thrills. We're attached to these things. When we're uncomfortable, we're not happy. And we run away from boredom, especially the boredom of being alone with ourselves.

We may think that simply because we can choose how we will spend our weekend, we are free. But this is not freedom, not when we are unable to face what we are or to be with life as it is. We are not free when our life is run by the search for pleasure and the avoidance of discomfort.

Freedom is unflinching attention to what's happening in our everyday life. Freedom is being with our thoughts and feelings, no matter how difficult or painful they may be. Loneliness, depression, fear, humiliation—when we can experience these as they arise and for as long as they continue, without having to change them, then we are truly free.

We can be dominated by the thought "Life is not as it should be." The consequence of this is anger. Anger can be extremely deep, extremely pervasive, in us. We're angry that life isn't the way we want it to be.

Life is difficult, and we don't like that. We're exasperated about that. We want something else. A deep-seated irritation can run our life. A minor frustration can seem like the end of the world: one of the kids messes up the living room we just cleaned; a co-worker's mistake creates extra work for us; a forgotten bill comes due; our arthritis kicks up again.

The result is that we're unhappy. We react to our problems out of irritation, and so we don't respond properly to them; we only make them worse. We could deal far more effectively with our difficulties if we would not react to them out of irritation.

To be aware means that we watch our frustration as soon as it comes up, without judging it. "Oh, I know I'm irritated; I'll just be with it for as long as it lasts." We experience its physical sensations: a knot in the stomach, a tightness in our shoulders. We watch and experience it all, instead of rationalizing it. This will feel like a dying process. But it is the only way to freedom. It allows the frustration to fade away, rather than dominate our life.

The frustration we experience when "life is not as it should be" permeates everything, even our relationships. We expect our spouse to be in a good mood, our children to be obedient, our boss to be pleasant, our friend to be supportive. When they are not, we become impatient. "He is not as he should be. She is not the way I want her to be."

Our expectations about others are the cause of our troubles. These expectations come from the past. For example, our spouse may have seemed kind, sensitive, and selfless when we first met. And so we formed an image of him or her as Mr. Wonderful or Miss Bright Sunshine. But later on, after we've been married awhile, he or she fails to live up to that image, and we're disturbed. "You should be like the person I married, not like you are now," is our attitude.

The result is conflict, misery, a breakdown in communication, and resentment. Relationships are strained to the limit. Countless marriages and friendships break up because of this.

If we want healing in our relationships, we have to live with other people as they are, rather than as we want them to be. And we have to die to our resistance to this by watching our anger for as long as it continues. This awareness liberates us to be with life as it is, other people as they are. It is the key to genuine happiness.

It is easy to live life as a victim. When I don't get what I want, when my feelings are hurt, when things don't work out the way they should, I can feel victimized.

We seem to put a great deal of emphasis on feelings these days. How we feel has become critically important to us. If we're angry or hurt or sad, why, we're entitled to feel that way. We have a right to feel that way! And the world had better take notice that we feel the way we do! But this mindset tends to make us victims of our emotions. "I'm upset because I didn't get what I want; I'm hurt by what happened;

I'm angry about what you said." We allow these reactions to run our life. Our underlying thought is, "Everybody pay attention to me: I'm a victim. Everybody listen: Life has to do a full stop now because I'm upset."

This only centers the focus on me: how *I* feel, what *I* want. The situation that upset us doesn't get properly addressed because we're thinking about "me." What needs to be done isn't done because we're engrossed in "my" feelings.

There is nothing evil about having feelings or wants. The problem arises when we're attached to them—when we're unhappy because we don't get what we want, or when we allow ourselves to be victimized by our feelings. When we're attached to our wants and feelings, we're not free.

It's perfectly all right to have feelings of sadness or hurt or anger. But it is important that we experience those feelings nonjudgmentally, rather than justify them.

This can be an important insight if we're struggling with an addiction. One of the difficult things about addictions is that despite months or years of abstinence the addictive desire can remain with us. Just when we thought we'd conquered our habit, the desire to give in to it can recur, as strong as ever. Our reaction is, "I've worked so hard on this addiction. I should be free of it, I shouldn't be having this craving. This is not the way I want to be. There's something wrong with me!" And so we become discouraged. We feel that we're a victim of the recurring desire. This gives the addiction more energy. The only way to freedom is to pay attention to our thoughts, whatever they may be, without approving or disapproving of them—and to acknowledge when we don't. When we condemn our thoughts and desires, when we harbor the attitude "This should not be," we are enchained by our thoughts and feelings.

What we often fail to see is that we are victimized not by events and circumstances, but by our reaction to those events and circumstances. I remember hearing a war veteran remark, "You know, I was never offended when someone fired at me in combat, but I sure do get mad when I'm driving on the freeway and someone cuts in front of me in traffic." If we think about it, his comment is amazing. Few things in life would seem more "offensive" than another person deliberately trying to kill us. Yet this combat veteran, and probably many others like him, didn't experience it that way. Instead, he was offended by the actions of another driver on the freeway. His reaction was keyed to how he interpreted events: War is not personally offensive to me, but obnoxious behavior by other drivers is.

When we are upset, hurt, embarrassed, or frightened by something that happens to us, our challenge is to be with our thoughts and feelings about the event. It's not the event itself but our reaction to the event, our interpretation of what happened, that victimizes us.

When we can really see that people who do and say hurtful things to us are acting out of their own fear, insecurity, and inner violence, we are much more understanding. We have an example in Jesus, who asked that his executioners be forgiven, because "they know not what they do." The crucified Jesus shows us that while reality can at times seem tragic, it is never offensive. In other words, we don't need to take setbacks personally. As the biblical Job learned in his own encounter with suffering, we humans are not the center of the universe. We misinterpret things by thinking that any ordeal that comes our way is a personal slight, an offense against who we are. We make ourselves unhappy by holding the attitude that we've been wrongly singled out to endure this awful trial.

If we are willing to watch our reactions, we need not be a victim even in the worst of situations. If someone says something unkind to me and I become angry, my task is to live the moment, to be the anger. This means that I notice the anger as soon as it arises, that I observe it without judging it, so that there is no opposition, no distance between me and the anger. I watch the anger so closely that I *am* the anger. This prevents the anger from taking hold in me and ruining my day, running my life. This allows my mind to remain clear.

Some psychotherapy and self-help techniques involve substituting "positive" thoughts for negative ones. If I've had a hurtful or traumatic experience, I can block out this trying event by focusing on a memory of some pleasant or joyful experience I had in the past. Or I can think about an imaginary pleasant experience. If I suffer from a bad self-image, I can create a new, affirming image by telling myself that I'm good, wonderful, special.

These techniques may be helpful coping mechanisms, but they don't bring freedom. They forcibly replace one thought with another. The clash between the positive thought and the negative thought remains, even if it seems to be submerged and out of sight for a while.

We are capable of doing more than just coping with reality. Far more. We are capable of living with a powerful inner freedom "in any and all circumstances," as Saint Paul says (Philippians 4:12). This freedom is gained not by techniques or thinking, but by silent awareness.

To live in that stillness is certainly a great challenge, a challenge that we will probably never meet all of the time. We have to be enormously patient with ourselves here. When we realize that we're not being attentive, we simply take note of that and return our attention to the moment. We will have to do this time and time again. If we do, and if we have a discipline of awareness in our daily meditation or prayer (see

Appendix II), then slowly, over time, our awareness of the present moment will grow and grow.

Fundamentally, freedom is not freedom of choice. We are free to the extent that we can live the moment.

If I lose my job, can I live that moment, be with all the worry, the anxiety, the depression, it may bring? This can certainly be a demanding situation to deal with. But it is unfreedom, an inability to be with what is, which prompts me to escape this circumstance through alcohol or other means.

If one of my parents develops Alzheimer's disease and has to be placed in a nursing home, can I face that situation and continue to care for my parent? If I can't visit my parent in the nursing home because I find it too distasteful or inconvenient, I'm being run by my avoidance.

If I do something foolish or asinine in public and feel humiliated, can I live that incident and experience those feelings fully? I take away my freedom if I try to repress that event and pretend it didn't happen. On the other hand, if I can brave those feelings without evaluating them, they begin to disappear.

If I'm stuck in conversation with a person I find really obnoxious, someone I don't like at all, can I be fully present to that person? It is freedom that allows me to notice my feeling of dislike instead of being controlled by it.

Freedom means to live the moment and to live it fully, however difficult that may be. Freedom means that we face the moment and do what needs to be done, even though we may want to be doing something else.

An indicator of how free we are can be the amount of responsibility we assume in our life. If my home is a filthy mess, but I can't bring myself to clean it up, then I'm not free. Cleaning can take time, it's unpleasant, and I'd rather be a couch potato. This is my avoidance. To be run by my avoidance is like being in confinement. I'm not free to do what needs to be done.

So many marriages break up because one or both of the spouses aren't free to maintain the commitment. After the courtship and the first years of marriage, the blissful, in-love feelings wear off. We begin to realize that this beautiful wife or handsome husband we married is in fact a human being, with faults and failings. That secretary or co-worker at the office really begins to look attractive, and we think, "Well, I must have married the wrong person. This new person is so attractive to me. I should get a divorce." We can abandon our commitment, our responsibility to our marriage, because of our feeling of attraction toward someone else. But to be run by our feelings is not freedom.

We can view our personal life, our family life, as our private escape from the rest of the world. We have a job only so that we can earn money for our family, our own well-being. We barely know our neighbors. We become concerned about politics or government only when inflation or unemployment begin to affect our pocketbook. We can center our lives around our private time, time off, recreation. Our life can be controlled by the search for comfort and entertainment. We end up isolating ourselves in our own private world. The result is that we have little sense of connection with the rest of the planet. We aren't able to see our profound relationship with every human being, our oneness with the threatened environment in which we live.

Awareness is the only way to liberation. When we begin to be aware of how restrained and confined our life is, then our responsibilities become apparent. We get more and more clarity about what needs to be done, about what we need to do in this present moment in our home, our marriage, our relationships, our community. Freedom gives rise to commitment. The freer we are, the greater the sense of commitment we will have in our life.

"Not my will," Jesus prayed, "but yours be done" (Luke 22:42). Following "your Will" may not be a very appealing notion today. We tend to think it means conforming our lives to an alien will, enduring punishing self-denial, bending to an external command.

Yet God is not an external object to which we must bend our will. Christian theology has always taught that divine will and human freedom go together. The more we are truly free and alive, the more "your will be done" is true in our life. The more we allow "your will" to work in our lives, the freer we are.

Our deep-seated attitude that "life is not the way it should be" is the fundamental restraint on our lives. It's like a heavy chain around our neck, dragging us down and choking the life out of us. To drop this chain is to step into freedom. To let go of this heavy burden is to follow "your will."

In my ministry, I often find myself having to do things I'd rather not do. I don't like meetings, especially long ones, yet I attend a good number of them. I am not thrilled about doing administrative work, yet there is a good deal of that to do in parish ministry. I often find myself thinking, "I'd rather not be here. Can we get this over with?" When I allow that thinking to go unobserved by myself, it takes me out of the moment and drains my energy. I find myself caught in a continual struggle of trying to distance myself from what's happening.

If I can watch my resistance, however, it usually disappears. I find that I can quickly forget that I don't like doing this. I can lose myself in the moment. I have discovered that meetings can even be enjoyable once I've dropped my resistance.

"Blessed are the poor in spirit," Jesus said. The ultimate poverty of spirit is not to need the moment to be any different from what it is. We are poor in spirit when we don't demand that we do only things we want to do, when we don't require that we be around only those people we like. We are poor in spirit when we don't insist on having pleasant thoughts and good feelings in our mind all the time. So when we're anxious, we can be the anxiety. When we're depressed, we can watch the depression. When we feel uncomfortable, we can be fully with the discomfort.

When we don't desire that we have any particular state of mind, when we are able to be with our thoughts and feelings no matter what they are, when we are able to live each moment as it is, whatever it may be, then our life is "your will be done." And then we are truly free, free from self.

The resurrected Christ confirms that reality offers ultimate healing and liberation, if we can be with it. To abandon ourselves to the real is the only way to this liberation. To live with what is means never to be a victim of life. To surrender to "your will" is to live in freedom.

Now some people might interpret this to mean that we should be passive in the face of whatever happens to us, no matter how unjust or hurtful it is. But that is incorrect. Dropping our resistance to being with what is does not turn us into a doormat. It does not mean that we are to be stepped on or abused by others.

I once knew a woman who for years endured abuse from her husband. Fear kept her in this awful situation: fear of incurring his wrath if she defied him, fear of not being able to make it on her own if she were to leave him. Finally, she realized how hopeless and damaging her situation was. She packed her bags and left. A local support agency found her a safe house where she could stay. She wrote her husband a note telling him to seek counseling, to get help, or else the marriage would be finished. This was a very brave move on her part, and it was something she was able to do only after she faced her fear.

In my own life, I've found that when I can be with what's actually happening, when I'm not resisting the moment, a real wisdom seeps in; I know what I need to do in whatever situation I'm in. Jesus told us not to worry about what we are to say and do. We will find the wisdom to do what needs to be done if we have the faith to let go and experience the moment.

I've often been asked, "If we're only living the present moment, how can we plan anything? In my job, I have to think about the future, I have to do a lot of planning. How can I do that and live the moment?"

Present-moment living doesn't mean that we neglect the future. Rather, it means that we don't see the future as bringing us more happiness than we have now. We don't see it as a time when we'll be happier than we can be in this present moment. So when we're planning a five-year project, we can be fully present to all that we do as we plan the project. But we're not planning to be more happy in five years than we are now. It's a question of where we are psychologically. To live the moment means that we're psychologically living in the here and now, not condemning ourselves for the past or worried about the future. That's the daily invitation to all of us.

27

A Moment of Grace

~

Throughout life we await the coming of the Lord in our everyday routines, and at the end of time. That last appearance might pose a problem for us. The thought of a Final Judgment can be a disturbing prospect of the future, something about which we're afraid or nervous. Or perhaps we reject altogether the idea of a Last Judgment, thinking that a loving God would never hold such a threat over our heads.

People have been grappling with the notion of a Last Judgment for thousands of years. The ancient Egyptians had a rather frightening image of it. In their *Book of the Dead*, the god Osiris and forty-two surrounding deities were pictured as seated in judgment over any person who passed to the next life. Each of these deities was responsible for detecting a specific sin. There were gigantic weighing scales in the scene, standing next to which was a divine scribe who would record the result of the judicial proceedings. Next to the divine scribe stood a monster with the head of a crocodile. It was the monster's job to devour all those whose good deeds did not prove heavy enough to outweigh their bad deeds.[1]

Many religions believe in a Final Judgment; and for most, the Last Judgment is a threat, a menacing prospect.

What about Christians? What do Christians believe about the Judgment? Saint Paul tells us that Christ died for us; that Christ took on our sins and died the death of a sinner once for all; and that where sin abounds, grace abounds all the more. (See Romans 5:8; 6:10; 5:20; 2 Corinthians 5:21.) For Christians, the Final Judgment is a moment of grace, not one of fearful damnation.

Judgment is a blessing, an honor for us. Judgment is an act of grace because it shows that God cares, cares deeply about us and about our lives.

There's a story about an American family. The father was a serviceman whose plane was shot down over North Vietnam during the Vietnam War. He was captured and became a prisoner of war, leaving behind a wife and a six-month-old son. He was a POW for eight years. As his young son grew, he learned about his father and how he had become a prisoner of war, and how someday he might be freed and allowed to return home. The boy heard his mother talk lovingly of his father, and he longed to see him. But he also had questions about him. "Will my father love me?" he thought. The boy had seen how the fathers of some of his playmates behaved, how they yelled and screamed at their children and even beat them. "Will my father be that way with me?" the boy wondered.

Finally, after eight long years, the news came that his father was soon to be released from captivity. The boy was excited but also a bit apprehensive about meeting the father he had never really known.

The boy and his mother met the father at the airport. The father embraced them both. As they returned home, and over the following days, the little boy was repeatedly surprised to find that his father wanted to know all about him. He wanted to know all that had happened to him during these past eight years. He wanted to learn how his life was going right now. The child had never realized that someone could care so much about him. The father wanted to know how well the boy had been doing in school. He told his son, "Your grades are not bad, but I think you could work harder too." He also told him, "You could do more to help your mother around the house, you know." And the boy knew that his father was right about the things he was saying. His father's words were challenging, even discomforting, to him, but he was very happy to learn that he had a father who cared that much about him.

Like that boy's encounter with his father, the Last Judgment is a blessing, not a curse. It's a blessing because it means that God is deeply concerned about us and our lives.

Imagine if there were no Final Judgment. If there were no Last Judgment, God would be saying, in effect, "I don't care! I don't care that sin and evil exist. I don't care that people are suffering and oppressed, that people are hurt by greed and brutality. I don't care about your life, about your struggles, your failures, your hurts, your joys. I'm indifferent to it all. It means nothing to me."

What kind of God would that be? Certainly not the God whom Christians worship, not the God of Jesus Christ.

The fact that God judges human history means that our human affairs have dignity, that God takes it all seriously. The fact that God judges my life means that my life is valued, divinely valued. Our lives are infinitely important because the Lord of the universe cares enough about us to deem our lives significant.

The Last Judgment is not a threat, not something that should make us afraid or anxious. "OK," we think, "that's all well and good, but there's still going to be a *judgment*, isn't there? We're still going to be judged."

Some saints and mystics have spoken about their experience of God as an encounter with overwhelming light, a light so brilliant that it's not possible for the human eye to look at it. Our eyes are accustomed to living in the dim world of self-centeredness, the shadows of our original sin. When we encounter God, the light is so bright that there's nowhere to hide, no way to cover up who we truly are. Our sin, our selfishness, our attachments, are all exposed and illuminated. We can't live in denial anymore. That's the Judgment. In fact, it's a judgment of light, not condemnation.

The old notion of purgatory is important here. Purgatory is not a place of punishment. It's not a place at all. Purgatory is a *process*. It's a process of purification, a process of growing enlightenment, a process of letting go of all of those things that keep us living in the shadows.

In fact, purgatory is a process that begins now, in this life. Each of us knows how difficult, even painful, it can be to let go of things like anger and envy. It's hard to drop those things. To undergo that process is purgation. Our lives have such importance, such divine worth, that we are invited to join this great quest for illumination right now.

There's something more we need to know about judgment. In our civil courts, judgments are impersonal and objective. The judge isn't supposed to know or have any bias one way or another about the people he or she is judging. In the classic picture of the scales of justice, Justice is depicted as a woman who stands blindfolded next to the scales. She's blindfolded because she's impersonal and objective. She doesn't see the person who is judged. All she does is weigh the issues and the facts.

That's not the case with the Christian experience of Judgment. We have a personal judge, Jesus Christ, who cares greatly about us. And he's not blindfolded. He sees completely, fully. He's more intimate to us than we are to ourselves. He's not cold and objective. As John's Gospel says, "God did not send the Son into the world to condemn the world, but in order that the world might be saved through him" (John 3:17). Christ, our Judge, only wants to save us, love us, challenge us—not condemn us.

The only sad thing that could happen here is if we were to refuse this love, to choose not to treasure ourselves as much as God does, to reject God's concern for our life. Because God's Judgment is not something to be feared or anxious about. God's Judgment is truly a moment of grace.

Postscript

~

Fear has been a major obstacle to inner freedom in my life. Fear is perhaps the main barrier to union with the Divine. And so, for many years, my burning desire has been to let go of all fear. Since writing this book, I have experienced a certain marvelous fulfillment to that longing. I have discovered that truth and unconditional love are direct experiences of the Divine rather than beliefs; and that when we remain centered in this immediate experience there can be no fear. I have also found that it is extremely difficult to proclaim this message, and be correctly understood, in an official ministry setting in the Church. The message can quickly be lost or distorted in an institution that places so much emphasis on beliefs and teachings instead of direct experience. Therefore, for the time being, I have taken a leave of absence from the priesthood. However, I intend to continue to share with all who are interested the work of spiritual transformation and the possibility of life without fear.

Appendix I:

Some Practical Meditations

~

An Encounter With Your Elder

I magine that you see someone walking toward you. The person walking is *you* at the age of one hundred years. Your face is weathered, your body frail, but there is a grace and a glow about you. Your elder comes to you and says: "Everyone has told you, 'You must change, you must improve, you must be better, do this, do that, be this, be that.' I've come to tell you that it is all wrong. It doesn't bring you change or happiness. It leads nowhere. Give up this way. Drop it at once!" Stay with this encounter, perhaps closing your eyes as you do....Allow the elder's words to point you deep within yourself....See all the ways, big and small, that you are trying to become....What happens when you heed this advice, when you absolutely give up your desire to become?

Weeds in the Garden

Bring to mind something about yourself that you've been trying to change, but without success. Some habit, addiction, hurtful inclination, or unseemly aspect of yourself that you would like to eliminate from your life. Observe your negative judgments about it: your dislike or hatred of it, your condemnation of it, your shame or disgust about it. Realize that these reactions are all just thoughts.

Now, look at the addiction, habit, or tendency firsthand, with no judgment or conclusion. Examine it as you would a fascinating piece of rock. See it deeply: the thrill or good feeling you may get from it; the fear or insecurity that may be underneath it; all of the denial and cover-up; the repression of it; the preoccupation with it; its harmful effects, physical and emotional; how it keeps you from having to face silence, pain, or emptiness in your life; and how it ultimately arises from self-disdain. Be with this desire or addictive tendency without evaluating it or trying to change it.

Ideals

On a separate sheet of paper, or in the appropriate column below, list all the ideals that you are striving to achieve—for example, goodness, kindness, loving person, perfect parent, sinless Christian, impressive or successful person, and so on. Then tally the price you pay for trying to be these ideals: the fear, the guilt, the shame, the energy drain, the loss of freedom and spontaneity, the judgmentalism, the blindness to what's actually true about you. Then list the perks you receive from identifying with these ideals: the self-righteousness, the comfort of not having to face what's actually true about you. Now look at the total price you are paying and ask yourself, "Do these perks justify this cost? Am I willing to let go of chasing after these ideals?"

Ideals I am trying to become:	The price I pay:	The perks I receive:

The Real

After you have completed the ideals meditation, describe or acknowledge what's really true about you. Be bluntly honest here, especially in those areas where previously you may have been blind about yourself because of your ideals. Do this in a nonjudgmental way, without evaluating yourself as good or bad.

Once you've finished, decide if there are any actions you now realize you should take: an apology to make, a relationship to heal through a new communication from you, some damage to repair....

Breathing Exercise

(This is an exercise that I received from Thich Nhat Hanh. It can be used with any troubling or difficult emotion, such as fear, anger, or depression.)

Allow yourself to be present to what it is you are thinking and feeling. Notice the physical sensations that are part of your fear or your anger, for example the tightness, the tenseness, or the ache in your body. As you experience all that, breathe with it in this way:

As you inhale, say silently to yourself, "Breathing in, I acknowledge that I am angry (or afraid, or depressed, and so on)."

As you exhale, say silently to yourself, "Breathing out, I embrace my anger." As an alternative, you can say, "Breathing out, I accept my anger," or "Breathing out, I smile," or any other words you want to use that will enable you to be with, and breathe with, the feeling.

As you continue to breathe, you may find it helpful to abbreviate what you say silently on the in-breath and out-breath. For example, on the in-breath, you can simply say to yourself, "Anger," and on the out-breath you can say, "Embrace."

When you breathe with strong emotions, and the thoughts that accompany them, they begin to lose their power, and they may even disappear altogether. It's often amazing how quickly this breathing exercise can bring peace and joy.

Appendix II:

Methods of Listening Prayer

~

Breathing Prayer and Centering Prayer

Centering prayer is not just a method of being intent on a sacred word. Breathing prayer is not just a way of being attentive to bodily sensations in breathing. Each of these prayers is a surrender of our entire being to God. Each is a way of emptying ourselves so that we may be fully open to God's healing, transforming grace. These prayers of silence gradually empty our unconscious of the wounds and baggage of the past, and move us toward union with Ultimate Reality, the God who is beyond our thoughts, ideas, and images.

It's best not to try to make a practice of doing both prayers. To do that is like drilling a number of wells, none of them very deep. Instead, choose the one prayer that suits you best, and stay with that. Allow it to take you deep within, where the reign of God is to be found.

If you can, do the prayer twice a day—for example, morning and evening—for about twenty or twenty-five minutes each time. Try to do it at the same time each day. If you don't have the time to do it twice a day, then do it once a day, at least for ten or fifteen minutes.

Centering Prayer[1]

Sit comfortably in a chair, keeping your back straight. (You can also sit in any one of the prayer postures described for the breathing prayer below.) Choose a sacred word of one or two syllables, such as "Spirit" or "Creator," or another word you prefer. It is better to choose a word that does not stir up memories or emotions in your mind. The sacred word is only an expression of your intent to be fully present to God. The less the word means to you, the better off you are. The word establishes a silent openness within you that helps you to move in pure faith toward God.

Close your eyes. To slow down the usual flow of thoughts, think just one thought: the sacred word. To start, introduce the sacred word in your imagination as gently as if you were laying a feather on a piece of absorbent cotton. Keep thinking the sacred word in whatever form it arises. You don't have to repeat it continuously. The word can flatten out, become vague or just an impulse of the will, or even disappear. Accept it in whatever way it arises.

When you become aware that you are thinking some other thought, return to the sacred word as the expression of your intent. The effectiveness of this prayer does not depend on how distinctly you say the sacred word or how often, but rather on the gentleness with which you introduce it into your imagination in the beginning and the promptness with which you return to it when you are hooked on some other thought.

Thoughts are an inevitable part of centering prayer. Our ordinary thoughts are like boats sitting on a river so closely packed together that we cannot see the river that is holding them up. We are normally aware of one object after another that passes across our inner screen of consciousness: images, memories, feelings, external impressions. When we slow down that flow for a little while, space begins to appear between the boats. Up comes the reality on which they are floating.

Centering prayer is a method of directing your attention from the particular to the general, from the concrete to the formless. At first you are preoccupied by the boats that are going by. You become interested in seeing what is on them. But just let them all go by. If you catch yourself becoming interested in them, return to the sacred word as the expression of the movement of your whole being toward God present within you.

The sacred word is a simple thought that you are thinking at ever-deepening levels of perception. That's why you accept the sacred word in whatever form it arises within you. The word on your lips is exterior and has no part in this form of prayer. The thought in your imagination is interior; the word as an impulse of your will is more interior still. Only when you pass beyond the word into pure awareness is the process of interiorization complete. That is what Mary of Bethany was doing at the feet of Jesus. She was going beyond the words she was hearing to the Person who was speaking and entering into union with him. This is what we are doing as we sit in centering prayer and interiorize the sacred word. We are going beyond the sacred word into union with that to which it points—the Ultimate Mystery, the Presence of God, beyond any perception that we can form of God.

The Breathing Prayer[2]

Sit in one of the prayer postures described below. Now be fully aware of your breathing. Pay attention only to your inhalation when breathing in, and only to your exhalation when breathing out. Receive each in-breath as a gift. Surrender yourself completely to each out-breath. Be one with your breathing in each present moment.

To help maintain your alertness, you may find it helpful to count each breath. Count only from 1 to 10, and then start over again. Count the in-breaths on the odd numbers, 1, 3, 5, 7, 9, and the out-breaths on the even numbers 2, 4, 6, 8, 10. If you are distracted by thoughts, you may find it helpful to just count the in-breaths. If you are drowsy, count only the out-breaths.

Once you are able to maintain attentiveness in counting your breaths, you can simply focus your attention on your breathing without counting.

In this prayer, breathe through the nose, and deeply from the diaphragm. To do this, imagine that your nostrils are about two inches below the navel.

Breathe naturally, without any artificial pauses between breaths. Never hold your breath during this prayer.

During the breathing prayer, keep your eyes slightly open and focused on the floor about three feet directly in front of you. You don't need to think about anything that you might see. Keeping your eyes open will help to keep distracting thoughts from arising in your mind.

Do not judge or suppress thoughts or feelings that arise as you do the breathing prayer. Let them be, and return to the awareness of your breathing. If they are strong or persistent, simply breathe with them.

It's important to know that breathing can be a powerful

prayer. The Christian Zen teacher Ruben Habito notes that the word "spirituality" comes from the Greek word *pneuma*, or spirit, which in turn comes from the Hebrew *ruah*, the breath of God. In the Old Testament, the Breath of God plays a critical role in salvation history, beginning with creation itself (Genesis 1:2). In the New Testament, Jesus' entire life is marked by the presence of the Breath of God. He is conceived by this Spirit (Luke 1:35), and his life and ministry are anointed by the Spirit that is upon him (Luke 4:18-19). Habito says:

> In other words, the key to understanding the life of Jesus is in his being replete with the Breath of God; his whole existence is vivified, guided, inspired and fulfilled in it.[3]

Paying attention to our breath, Habito explains, can be an effective way of self-abandonment to the Breath of God here and now.

So, do not do the breathing prayer halfheartedly! This can be a profound way of surrendering to Ultimate Reality.

Postures for the Breathing Prayer

In every posture, sit with the spine straight, ears in line with the shoulders, and tip of the nose in line with the navel. The chin should be slightly drawn in.

Lotus Position: Sit on the front of a firm pillow or round cushion. While sitting, place the right foot on the left thigh, and the left foot on the right thigh, with both knees touching the floor or mat. Knees should be in line with each other, the abdomen relaxed and slightly protruded. Place the left hand, palm up, on top of the palm-up fingers of the right hand, with thumbs touching lightly to make an oval, hands resting on the feet. This is the Full-Lotus Position, the best position for Breathing Prayer. For many of us, months of stretching are required to be able to sustain this position. In the meantime, you may instead try the Half-Lotus Position: left foot over the right thigh, and right foot under the left thigh, both knees touching the floor or mat. Or the Quarter-Lotus Position: with the left foot resting on the calf of the right leg, both knees resting on the mat. Or the Burmese Position: with the legs uncrossed, the left or right foot in front and both knees resting on the mat.

I can't fully explain why, but somehow it's easier to keep our mind quiet and our attention focused when we're in the Lotus Position or one of its variations. However, it's not essential to be in that position. Don't force yourself into any of these positions if your body is not able or ready to do so. For many of us, months of stretching are required before we will be able to do the Lotus Position. You may instead want to use a prayer bench, or a chair. If you sit in a chair, try to keep your spine straight. You may find it helpful to place a cushion on the chair and, after you are seated, draw your feet in or to the side, so that you can lower your knees. The mind remains quieter when the knees are lower than the hips.

Notes

~

Chapter 1: The Desire to Become

1. Quoted in *The Snow Leopard* by Peter Matthiessen (New York: Viking Press, 1987), pp. 62-63.

2. Saint John of the Cross, *The Ascent of Mount Carmel*, Book One, Chapter 13, in *The Collected Works of John of the Cross*, revised edition, translated by Kieran Kavanaugh, O.C.D., and Otilio Rodriguez, O.C.D. (Washington, D.C.: ICS Publications, 1991), p. 150.

3. Meister Eckhart, quoted in *The Practice of Zen Meditation* by Hugo Enomiya-Lassalle (San Francisco: HarperCollins, 1992), p. 63.

4. Thomas Merton, *Asian Journal of Thomas Merton* (New York: New Directions, 1973), p. 308.

Chapter 2: How Do I Change?

1. Krishnamurti, the mystic from India, was perhaps the first one to point to the inner conflict between the ideal and the actual as the source of violence and war. He said, "War is the spectacular and bloody projection of our everyday life." Krishnamurti, *The First and Last Freedom* (New York: Harper & Row, 1954), p. 182.

2. Ruth Leger Sivard, *World Military and Social Expenditures 1991* (Washington, D.C.: World Priorities, 1991), p. 20.

3. Quoted in *Original Blessing* by M. Fox (Santa Fe: Bear & Company, 1983), p. 132.

Chapter 3: Turnaround

1. *Metanoeite* in the Greek New Testament, Matthew 3:2. This Greek word has an equivalent meaning to the Hebrew *tshuvah*.
2. *Paenitentiam agite* in Latin.
3. Quoted in *Lectionary Homiletics*, Vol. III, No. 1, December 1991, p. 14.

Chapter 4: The Really Good News

1. Donald Senior, "Understanding Jesus," *Church*, Winter 1993, p. 9.

Chapter 6: Self-Awareness

1. The analogy of the prison cell and the story of the fish in the ocean have been adapted from *Everyday Zen* by Joko Beck (San Francisco: HarperSanFrancisco, 1989), pp. 145-46, 148.

Chapter 8: Transforming Our Vision

1. Philip St. Romain, *Kundalini Energy and Christian Spirituality* (New York: Crossroad, 1991), p. 40.
2. D.E. Nineham, *Saint Mark, The Pelican New Testament Commentary* (New York: Penguin Books, 1979), p. 234.

Chapter 9: Healing Our Source Relationship

1. As far as I know, Werner Erhard was the first one to state this fact in such categorical terms.*
2. Anthony de Mello relates a slightly different version of the story in *The Heart of the Enlightened: A Book of Story Meditation* (New York: Doubleday, 1989), p. 180.

Chapter 11: Know Yourself

1. The eminent Old Testament theologian Gerhard von Rad has this to say about this passage from Jeremiah:

> If we understand Jeremiah correctly, the new thing is
> to be that the whole process of God's speaking and

humanity's listening is to be dropped. This road of listening to the divine will had not led Israel to obedience. Jahweh is, as it were, to by-pass the process of
speaking and listening, and to put his will straight into
Israel's heart. We should completely ignore the distinction between outward obedience and obedience of the
heart, for it scarcely touches the antithesis in Jeremiah's
mind...every page of Deuteronomy, too, insists on an
obedience which springs from the heart and conscience.
It is at this very point, however, that Jeremiah goes far
beyond Deuteronomy, for in the new covenant the
doubtful element of human obedience as it had been
known up to date drops out completely. If God's will
ceases to confront and judge humans from outside themselves, if God puts his will directly into their hearts,
then, properly speaking, the rendering of obedience is
completely done away with, for the problem of obedience only arises when human will is confronted by an
alien will. Now however, the possibility of such a con-
frontation has ceased to exist, for humans are to have
the will of God in their heart, and are only to will God's
will. What is here outlined is the picture of a new humanity, a humanity which is able to obey perfectly because of a miraculous change of its nature.

Gerhard von Rad, *Old Testament Theology* Volume Two (Lon-
don: SCM Press, 1965), pp. 213-14.

2. Soliloquiorum II, I, in *Patrologia Latina*, 32, 885.

3. *Interior Castle*, Second Mansions, translated and edited by E.
Allison Peers (New York: Doubleday/Image Books, 1989),
p. 52.

4. Ruth Leger Sivard, *World Military and Social Expenditures 1991*
(Washington, D.C.: World Priorities, 1991), p. 20.

Chapter 12: Death and New Life

1. See the article "Does Chaos Rule the Cosmos?" by Ian
Stewart, *Discover*, Vol. 13, November 1992, pp. 56ff.

Chapter 13: A Firsthand Faith

1. Anthony de Mello, *The Song of the Bird* (Anand, India:
Gujarat Sahitya Prakash, 1982), pp. 65-66.

2. Reports of Experiences, in *The Way to Contemplation* by Willigis Jäger (Mahwah, NJ: Paulist Press, 1987), pp. 108, 101, 105. This book is out of print.
3. *Dogmatic Constitution on the Church*, paras. 40-42.
4. Thomas Keating, *Open Mind, Open Heart: The Contemplative Dimension of the Gospel* (Rockport, MA: Element, 1991), p. 75.
5. Quoted in "The Journey Within" by John B. Healey, *America*, Vol. 170, No. 6, February 19, 1994, p. 16.

Chapter 14: The Silence of Unknowing
1. *The Ascent of Mount Carmel*, Book One, Chapter 4.
2. From the Resurrection Homily of Saint John Chrysostom.

Chapter 15. The True Shepherd
1. Ramana Maharshi, quoted in Stephen Mitchell, *The Gospel According to Jesus* (New York: HarperPerennial, 1991), p. 147.

Chapter 16: The Illusion of Separateness
1. Two distinguished quantum physicists put it this way:

> One is led to a new notion of unbroken wholeness which denies the classical idea of analyzability of the world into separately and independently existing parts... We have reversed the usual classical notion that the independent "elementary parts" of the world are the fundamental reality, and that the various systems are merely particular contingent forms and arrangements of these parts. Rather, we say that inseparable quantum interconnectedness of the whole universe is the fundamental reality, and that relatively independently behaving parts are merely particular and contingent forms within this whole.

D. Bohm and B. Hiley, "On the Intuitive Understanding of Nonlocality as Implied by Quantum Theory," *Foundations of Physics*, Vol. 5 (1975), pp. 96, 102.
2. Thomas Merton, *Conjectures of a Guilty Bystander* (New York: Doubleday, 1966) pp. 140-42; quoted in *Living With Wisdom:*

A Life of Thomas Merton by Jim Forest (Maryknoll, New York: Orbis, 1991), p. 122.

Chapter 17: One in the Spirit

1. The editorial, which contains the remarks of Professor Lieberman, is entitled "What If World Had No Racial Groups? Scientists Are Finding That's the Case," by Joan Beck, *The Spokesman Review*, March 15, 1991, reprinted from *The Chicago Tribune*.

Chapter 18: The Ripple Effect

1. From Dogen (1200–1253 C.E.), *Shobogenzo*, quoted in *The Three Pillars of Zen* by Roshi Philip Kapleau (New York: Doubleday, 1989), p. 310.
2. From Walt Whitman, "Song of Myself," quoted in *The Sun My Heart: From Mindfulness to Insight* by Thich Nhat Hanh (Berkeley: Parallax Press, 1988), p. 67.
3. See Fritjof Capra, *The Tao of Physics: An Exploration of the Parallels Between Modern Physics and Eastern Mysticism* (Boston: Shambhala New Science Library, 2nd ed., 1985).

Chapter 19: Present-Moment Living

1. Hugo Enomiya-Lassalle, *Living in the New Consciousness* (Boston: Shambhala, 1988). See pp. 1-33.
2. Acts 1:11 refers to the *parousia*, or future coming of Christ. It is not my intention here to discuss eschatology. My chief concern is to examine how we can find life in abundance here and now.
3. Jack Kornfield, *A Path With Heart: The Perils of Spiritual Life* (New York: Bantam Books, 1993), p. 92.

Chapter 20: Listening to the Inner Voice

1. Joko Beck and Steve Smith, *Nothing Special, Living Zen* (San Francisco: HarperSanFrancisco, 1993), p. 99.

Chapter 21: The God of the Now

1. Paul J. Wharton, ed., *Stories and Parables for Preachers and Teachers* (New York: Paulist Press, 1986), p. 39.

2. I received this poem on a xeroxed sheet which was mailed to me by a friend. There was no indication that the poem had ever been published. I have since inquired and searched, but have not found the poem in any published work.

Chapter 24: "God Help Us If We Got What We Deserve!"

1. This quotation is taken from a 1985 edition of *The Catholic Worker* newspaper, but I have not been able to find the exact edition and page.

Chapter 25: The Dark Night

1. This story is told by Thomas Keating in *Invitation to Love* (Rockport, MA: Element, 1992), p. 81.
2. "The Living Flame of Love," stanza 3, #73, from *The Collected Works of St. John of the Cross*, translated by Kieran Kavanaugh, O.C.D., and Otilio Rodriguez, O.C.D. (Washington, D.C.: ICS Publications, 1991), pp. 53-54.

Chapter 27: A Moment of Grace

1. This information is taken from the article "The Last Judgment As an Act of Grace," by Eberhard Jungel, *Louvain Studies* 15 (1990), 389-405. A few of the ideas presented in that article have inspired this chapter.

Appendix II

1. This description of centering prayer is excerpted and paraphrased from *Open Mind, Open Heart: The Contemplative Dimension of the Gospel* by Thomas Keating (Rockport, MA: Element, 1991), pp. 110-11.
2. For more information about the breathing prayer, see *The Practice of Zen Meditation*, by Fr. Hugo Enomiya-Lassalle (San Francisco: Thorsons, 1991). This book also contains some stretching exercises that can be helpful for gaining the flexibility needed to sit in the lotus position.
3. Ruben L. F. Habito, *Total Liberation: Zen Spirituality and the Social Dimension* (Maryknoll, NY: Orbis, 1989), p. 105.

About the Author

~

Terence Grant formerly ministered as a priest for the Diocese of Spokane, Washington. He was a parish priest for eleven years, including five years as a pastor. Prior to ordination, he practiced law for several years as an attorney in Spokane. Grant received his theology degree from the Catholic University of Louvain in Leuven, Belgium. He studied Zen under *sensei* Ruben Habito at the Maria Kannon Zen Center in Dallas, Texas. Currently he lives in Santa Fe, New Mexico, where he does spiritual counseling and polarity therapy, and gives retreats and workshops dealing with spiritual awakening and transformation.